Charles Cruft's
Dog Book

Foreword by Dennis McCarthy

W. Foulsham & Co. Ltd.
London · New York · Toronto · Cape Town · Sydney

W. Foulsham & Co. Ltd.
Yeovil Road, Slough, Berkshire, SL1 4JH

ISBN 0-572-01208-X

© W. Foulsham & Co. Ltd.
This Revised Edition © Text and Illustrations 1983
W. Foulsham & Co. Ltd.

Cover illustration: Cocker Spaniel
(page 59) and Bernese Mountain Dogs (page 52).
Transparency supplied by Anne Cumbers, Reigate.

Photoset in Great Britain by
Rowland Phototypesetting Limited,
Bury St Edmunds, Suffolk
and printed in Hong Kong.

Contents

Foreword   4
The home dog   5
Choosing your dog   7
Housing and equipment   12
Puppy rearing   17
Puppy training   19
The dog's day   26
Feeding   28
Travelling   31
Illnesses   34
Boarding kennels   38
Breeding   40
Specially trained dogs   42
How much it costs   47
Major breeds   48
Index   95

Foreword

Here is a gem! A book written by Charles Cruft, grandson of the man who founded the famous dog show that bears his name.

What shines through this book is the man's respect for the dog. And a dog didn't have to have a top pedigree to gain that respect.

Too many dog books today print theory as fact. And I have argued with so many 'experts' about their theories. No fanciful theories here, but good solid fact. This is a book to read and read again, and to have by you all the time you have a dog.

Dennis McCarthy

1983.

Dennis McCarthy

The home dog

'Man's best friend is his dog.' The saying is as true today as ever it was, and perhaps more so in view of the age in which we live; moreover, it has been true since the far-distant days of the Stone Age.

Why did our prehistoric ancestors first keep dogs? Well, basically for the same reason that you and I keep a family pet: as a companion for the family and as a protector. In time the dog came to be trained as a worker, and breeding became a business matter. For thousands of years the dog has played a varied part in man's daily life.

As a companion the dog has no equal. Through fair weather and foul, he is just the same: he is incredibly faithful at all times, will stick to you through thick and thin, and demands little in return beyond his food, exercise and affection. The thing that probably means more to him than anything else is a little praise; it is good to make a habit of praising him whenever he is on good behaviour. This is, by the way, quite a different matter from affectionate small talk. Both praise and companionable talk satisfy a real canine need.

Wanting a dog for companionship covers a very wide field indeed, from the little old lady who loves to nurse her toy dog to the gamekeeper who thinks the world of his Springer Spaniel and asks no more than to have him at his side when doing his rounds.

You may, of course, want a dog for more than companionship alone, and in this case you will not have quite so many breeds to choose from. For instance, today many people quite rightly need a dog for protection in some form or another. Now though this means that you will be looking to certain breeds for certain qualities, it must not be interpreted as referring only to German Shepherd Dogs and large breeds akin to them. The little Sealyham or Dachshund can be a very good watch dog as far as sounding the alarm: so do bear this in mind if you are trying to make up your mind about choosing a dog. At this stage, however, we are concerned with why you want a dog. The choice of breed will be developed later.

It may well be that you want a dog for a person without sight or hearing, which means a companion, protector, and guide – a very good reason for wanting a dog. I should so like to see every one of the blind with a trained dog; but unfortunately there are several hundred men and women waiting for a dumb friend to share their lives, and this of course is because so few dogs are suitable for the purpose, and also the dogs have to undergo many weeks of training before being able to fulfil their excellent task.

Another common domestic need for a dog is as a companion for a child or children. I suppose in the average British home with a couple of children, the dog is more often than not the fifth member of the family. Providing the child is not too young (it is difficult to make a very young child understand that it must not tease or hurt the dog), a puppy can be a great educational factor in a child's upbringing. Children and dogs seem to me to have a common understanding, which is often quite beyond our comprehension. We will, however, take up this large subject of dogs and children again further on.

What do we eventually expect of our chosen dog? Whatever breed, large or small, young or old, the dog will sooner or later answer all our demands if we play our proper part: this depends very largely upon our understanding and the way he is brought up and treated.

While we are dealing with the question of why, we must not leave the subject of the show dog without mention, as a number of people do buy a dog for this express purpose alone. I think this is a mistake to a great extent; because if this is made the primary reason, surely companionship, intelligence, and other good qualities are being rather pushed into the background; and a dog is no showman without these essential qualities and many others. I know a man who (in common with a number of others) bought, at a very high price, a young potential show dog purely on its appearance and what he was told about it by a good salesman. The buyer had obviously been told there was a mint of money to be made in dog breeding and showing. The net result was that the new and delighted owner completely omitted to have the dog checked over by a veterinary surgeon or to inquire into its ancestry. The poor wretched animal suffered from ever-increasing fits, and was consequently useless for the purpose of showing or breeding. I am quite sure you are as capable of drawing the conclusion as I am, so we will leave it at that.

Choosing your dog

The choice of a dog or puppy is a very much more serious problem than merely discussing why we are going to have one. We have reached the practical stage here, and it is a matter that calls for some very serious thought, for the average length of life of a dog is in the region of twelve years, and there must be no question of a change of heart, unless for an absolutely unavoidable reason. I always contend that to change the ownership of a dog after he has reached the adult stage is almost as great a calamity as sending a child away to another family.

Let us return, then, to the choice. First of all the question of space. Is it to be a small dog for a small house and a big dog for a big house? Broadly speaking this is the way it should be, but it is not an inflexible rule. For example, I myself have found that a big breed such as, for example, a Great Dane or German Shepherd can be less trouble in a confined space than many of the small breeds, provided there is ample opportunity for exercise, particularly as most of the big breeds are very docile animals and will curl up in an incredibly small space – often artfully chosen before the fire, keeping everyone else at a considerable distance. I must, however, agree with my wife that having a St Bernard in our cottage was rather beyond a joke, to say nothing of what happened on a wet day!

The big breed is normally a good guard dog, and the intruder is more readily deterred by the appearance of a dog weighing upwards of 27 kilograms (60 lb), to say nothing of the bark that goes with it. The small fellows are, of course, very courageous and I am not suggesting that it is essential to have a big dog for protection. I only wish to point out that the choice must be an individual matter.

The chances are that you will be having a puppy rather than an adult. A youngster is the obvious choice because it is most desirable to train him yourself and get him used to your own particular circumstances at the earliest possible age. There is some difference of opinion as to the age at which the puppy should leave the litter, and for my part I think eight weeks is quite soon enough. I have heard so many people say, 'But they have been feeding themselves for the last three weeks.' This may be so, but nevertheless the litter need the comfort of one another for as long as possible – and also the breeder needs ample opportunity for worming them, and giving an eye to them generally.

Another important aspect in choosing a puppy, assuming that you have decided which breed it is to be, is the question of where he is coming from – a breeder? a pet shop? or someone advertising in the local paper? Strange though it may seem, it is unwise to trust your own judgement of any of these unless you have been recommended to them or they are well known to you by reputation. The local veterinary surgeon can, of course, give some very useful advice on this subject.

I have known so many people who have been unlucky in buying a dog during the past few years that I do seriously ask you to stop and think very carefully before getting a cheap puppy. Plenty are advertised, but you can easily buy a load of trouble by paying a very low price for a pedigree puppy. On reflection you will realise that to feed the bitch well before the birth of the puppies and to raise them properly to the selling age cannot be done if they are to be sold at too cheap a price. Something must have been omitted to make this selling price possible, and you may well find that you pay this amount again in veterinary bills during the first year. Prices vary, of course, both between and within breeds, but you will find some cost guidelines on page 47. In my opinion a good puppy is quite the best investment in the world: he is not difficult to get, costs very little to maintain, and will give you great joy and companionship for probably some twelve years. What more can you expect for your initial outlay?

I have heard it said, 'Oh, I cannot be bothered with a puppy. Let's have one a year old that is clean and more settled in his ways.' With only a few exceptions this attitude is a mistake, and not to be recommended. A dog soon gets attached to a home, and it is a bad thing to change an adult dog over to a new home, except in cases where an animal has been ill-treated or a lost dog is taken from a dogs' home.

All dogs are attractive in one way or another and this particularly applies to puppies. Different breeds often look very much alike when they are anything up to eight weeks of age; but for goodness' sake never be misled by this when making your choice. If, for various reasons, you decide to have a cross-bred instead of a pedigree dog, you must beware of having one sold to you as a terrier type that will eventually grow into a gun dog cross or something even larger.

Many people prefer a pedigree dog, in whose appearance they can take pride, and which can be compared with others of the same breed. But out of the millions of dogs in Britain there are many thousands of mixed ancestry. (Call them mongrels if you like, but I prefer the term 'cross-breeds'.) This great band of nondescripts can and do offer to their owners just as much in companionship, and for that matter intelligence too, but taken overall those of very high intelligence are in the minority. I have personally been instrumental in placing many cross-breeds in good homes, but in practically every case the parents on each side have been known to me: in other words, we have had some idea of what the puppy was going to grow

BREED GOLDEN RETRIEVER
SEX DOG GOLDEN
COLOUR & MARKINGS GOLDEN
DATE OF BIRTH 2. 4. 71.
BREEDER MRS. P. L HEAVEN

KENNEL CLUB No. 35258/71
DATE OF REGISTRATION 23. 4. 71.
KENNEL CLUB STUD No.
OWNER
ADDRESS

pedigree

NAME OF DOG COFASTRE BARON

PARENTS	GRANDPARENTS	GREAT GRANDPARENTS	GT:GT: GRANDPARENTS	GT:GT:GT: GRANDPARENTS
SIRE — Name: INTERNATIONAL CHAMPION CABUS BOLTBY COMBINE; Kennel Club No. 2383/63; Name and Address of Owner: MRS. Z M. MCRARTY, GREYSTONES, BURTON LANE - BROUGHTON, PRESTON. LANCS.	Sire INTERNATIONAL CHAMPION CABUS CADET	Sire BEAUCHASSE JASON	Sire SOLWAY LADDIE	Sire CH. BEAUCHASSE DOMINIE
				Dam PRIMROSE QUEEN
			Dam BEAUCHASSE IMPRINT	Sire BOLTBY KYMBA
				Dam SH CH BEAUCHASSE BERGAMOT
		Dam BRECKLANDS TAMARIS	Sire BRECKLANDS REPORTER	Sire CH. ALRESFORD ADVERTISER
				Dam BRECKLANDS PRISCILLA
			Dam BRECKLANDS SHANI OF BREYDONVALE	Sire CH. RUSHLIGHT ROGER
				Dam KULDANA SHARLAND SHANI
	Dam SHOW CHAMPION BOLTBY SUGAR BUSH	Sire CHAMPION BOLTBY SKYLON	Sire BOLTBY KYMBA	Sire SH CH TORRDALE KIM OF STENBURY
				Dam DORCAS LEELA
			Dam BOLTBY SWEET MELODY	Sire TORRDALE DON JUAN
				Dam TORRDALE MELODY
		Dam BOLTBY GILLRAIN GALALINDA	Sire CHAMPION BOLTBY MOONRAKER	Sire BOLTBY KYMBA
				Dam BOLTBY SUNSHINE
			Dam GILLRAIN SUSAN	Sire TORRBRYN ARISTOCRAT
				Dam GLISGURGLISH LASSIE
DAM — Name: COFASTRE SWEET SMILER; Kennel Club No. 44 674/68; Name and Address of Owner: MRS. P. L. HEAVEN. CUCKOOS NEST FARM, STOKE GOLDING. NUNEATON. WARWICKS.	Sire HUGHENDEN CABUS COLUMBA	Sire CHAMPION CAMROSE TALLYRAND OF ANBRIA	Sire CHAMPION CAMROSE FANTANGO	Sire DORCAS TINGSICOMBE TEIFFER
				Dam CULDEN CATHASE TESS
			Dam CHAMPION JANE OF ANBRIA	Sire CH WILLIAM OF WESTLEY
				Dam CH BRIAR OF ARBROOK
		Dam CABUS BOLTBY CHARMER	Sire INTERNATIONAL CHAMPION CABUS CADET	Sire BEAUCHASSE JASON
				Dam BRECKLANDS TAMARIS
			Dam SHOW CHAMPION BOLTBY SUGAR BUSH	Sire CH BOLTBY SKYLON
				Dam BOLTBY GILLRAIN GALALINDA
	Dam COFASTRE GLENNESSA WOOD GOSSIP	Sire INTERNATIONAL + SWEDISH CHAMPION GLENNESSA WATERBIRD OF STENBURY	Sire WATER WIZARD OF STENBURY	Sire SH CH. BOLTBY SYRIAN
				Dam SH CH. WATERSPRITE OF STENBURY
			Dam SHOW CHAMPION WATERNYMPH OF STENBURY	Sire CH. BOLTBY SKYLON
				Dam SH CH. WATERWITCH OF STENBURY
		Dam CHAMPION GLENNESSA SEASPRITE OF STENBURY	Sire GLENNESSA CROFTER OF EMPSHOTT	Sire CH. BOLTBY SKYLON
				Dam GLENNESSA ALEXA
			Dam WATERSONNET OF STENBURY	Sire WATERSON OF STENBURY
				Dam SH CH. WATERNYMPH OF STENBURY

into, which is the most important thing when choosing a dog.

A word about pedigrees. The English Kennel Club is the organising body in the dog world in England, and other countries have similar bodies. The Kennel Clubs license all official dog shows, and also set the standards for all the breeds of dog. In addition to this, they maintain a record of every pedigree dog's life history; and to prove your own dog's pedigree you have only to write to this organisation to find out whether the document is authentic. This is an important thing to do, as pedigrees have been known to be false, particularly where dogs have been bought in markets. Here we have a good reason to support the well-known and established breeders who have a reputation to look after.

When a pedigree is handed over to you by the breeder, it may be that your particular dog has not been registered with the Kennel Club. Most breeders like to register their litters before selling them, but this is not always the case. Again, the document may show the sire registered and the dam not. Do not think because of this you are getting a cross-breed – the dam is probably quite a good specimen which the owner has not troubled to register. Anyway, if you are in doubt consult the Kennel Club, whose word is law on this subject.

Many people are rather baffled by a pedigree, which I must say can look a formidable piece of paper, particularly if some four generations are shown upon it. However, the example on page 9 shows you the way the dog's ancestry is set out, and will give you some idea and guidance when buying your puppy.

There is one very important thing to do before accepting a puppy from any source, and that is to get a veterinary certificate of a clean bill of health. An experienced dog handler may spot in an instant a flaw in the puppy's make-up that would quite naturally escape the layperson, so take good advice and get the opinion of a professional.

There are many things involved in choosing your dog, and to clarify the position still further let us look into the home of Mr and Mrs Smith and their two children. The family lives in a pleasant suburban semi-detached house with normal accommodation and a nice garden behind. The children have been worrying their parents for a considerable time for a puppy of their own, and they are five and seven years old respectively. The subject has been cropping up for many months and has been thrashed out in detail. Now it is almost Christmas (not really a perfect time of year to acquire a puppy), the parents feel that it is time to give in to the children's wishes, and they have the good sense to appreciate the value of a pet to the children. Father is very worried about the garden and what it is going to look like after a dog has been running round for six months, and mother is expecting more housework on wet days.

However, the decision is made and it begins to look very much as though four dogs are going to be kept instead of one, for the boy wants a Wire Fox Terrier, the girl a Cocker Spaniel, father a

Labrador, and mother a Miniature French Poodle! Well, after very great discussion they decide to have a Welsh Corgi. In my opinion, the choice is a good one, although there are at least a dozen breeds that would have fitted very well into the Smith household. The reason I say this is a good choice is that a fairly small dog has been chosen, he has a short, trouble-free coat, is clean in his habits, does not require long walks, and has a reasonable appetite. He is a very sharp little house dog, and of course originates from Wales, and is a working dog. Some people are opposed to short-legged dogs, but I do not agree – there is a lot to be said for them, particularly when they are to live in circumstances like these.

You may find something to think about in the Smiths' problem if you are upon the verge of the same important decision yourself. Let us assume you have been to a dog show at some time or another and know something of what most of the breeds look like. In the chapter on 'Major breeds' on page 48 you will find a guide giving some outline of characteristics of popular breeds, and I hope it will be of help in making your choice.

If you have decided to acquire a cross-breed puppy – and I am certainly not deprecating this – do satisfy yourself that the parents are both small breeds if you are intent on having a small dog. Don't buy a puppy solely on his attractive looks: remember that, like a child, he does not stay that way for long. It is an adult dog who will be living for years in your household, and few real dog lovers would have the heart to turn out a much bigger dog than they bargained for, having raised him for a year from that attractive puppy stage.

It is essential to spend a little time in studying many breeds, as if you are sold a puppy purported to be crossed between a Spaniel and a Dalmatian you will at least be able to identify the unmistakable characteristics naturally shown in the puppy. There is, by the way, a tendency for a puppy to inherit rather more from the dam than from the sire, and this generally applies to its size among other things.

If, on the other hand, you have decided to buy a pedigree puppy, and are prepared to pay a reasonable price for it, you should expect and get a dog to match the standards laid down for the specific breed, a general guide to which is given in the chapter on 'Major breeds' on page 48.

Housing and equipment

Housing is no difficulty in relation to the dog: the housing problem is a human rather than a canine one. Thank goodness, however, gone are the days when the poor dog was confined to an outdoor kennel on a length of chain none too long, with as often as not a leaky roof over his head. Swiftly moving civilisation has included the dog in its progress and in most cases today your four-footed friend is housed indoors in complete comfort, the usual place being the kitchen, where it is generally warm. Mind you, I am not opposed to the dog being kennelled out of doors, and in some cases it is the best option, particularly with a big breed, or a dog that is completely obedient and does not have to be tied up at night.

Let us return to your particular problem and assume that you have made some provisional arrangement for your dog's housing and comfort. The chances are that this has taken the form of a new, round basket to be placed in the kitchen, and probably tucked under the table or in a corner where nobody will fall over it. I have no fault to find with this, except perhaps that as an alternative to a basket, which is full of nooks and crannies for dirt and germs, a wooden tray box, slightly raised off the ground and free from draughts, would do just as well, and would probably be much easier to scrub regularly.

Undoubtedly the kitchen is the best place for your dog to live in, and it must be permanent. By this I do not mean ban him completely from all other parts of the house. When he is old enough, by all means let him have his share of the living-room fire; it will probably be a very generous share too, if I know anything about the average dog. Bedrooms are barred – invading them is a very bad habit indeed. I am as fond of animals as anyone alive, but this I will not tolerate. It is so easy to spoil your puppy to start with, but do try to be firm with it and teach good habits from the beginning.

Having got him home get the box or basket in position, and line it with an old blanket or soft cloth which will wash easily and also be comfortable to lie on. This, remember, must be shaken out of doors each morning, and when not in use in the basket left out to air in the open. If he is a young puppy he will not have water beside his basket at the start, but just a small dish of milk at regular intervals between solid feeds.

A toy is a great interest to a new puppy and it will help considerably to settle him into his new surroundings. It can take the form of a rubber bone, an old slipper or one of the many rubber toys you can buy from your pet shop. During the first day or two this will help distract his attention from the fact of being away from the rest of the

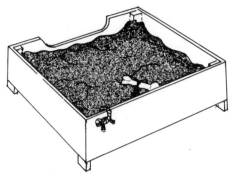

litter, and it is as well to tie the object to his basket by a length of cord. He is usually more interested in the latter, but this does not matter very much. All is well as long as he does not start on the new basket, as this is too costly to have mutilated by a mischievous puppy.

Another point about keeping him in the kitchen is that it is the best place to start training him to be clean and – just as important – to begin his training in being alert to callers, whom he should herald by barking even at an early age. Encourage this, but teach him also to understand the meaning of the word 'Quiet!'.

While we are on the subject of housing dogs indoors, there is another spot that many people find satisfactory and inconspicuous and that is under the stairs, if facilities are available; though I personally think the kitchen preferable.

Well now, a few words about the outdoors dog. He need be no less fortunate, and of course in the summer is far more fortunate, particularly if he has the right accommodation. Now just what do we mean by this? It seems a bit hard to leave a tiny puppy outside for the first night and I do not think it necessary. Very few people would do it, though if you have an accommodating cat for company it is a different matter; but he would have to be a very friendly cat indeed.

Let us then assume that you have decided the dog must live outside and he is not less than three or four months old. An elaborate kennel is probably the ideal answer; it is dry, roomy, and has a pleasant run adjoining. Needless to say, this is not absolutely necessary, even in a cheaper home-made edition; a small lean-to shed is perfectly satisfactory. The dog will be warm, dry and comfortable in it; it can be shut up last thing at night, with suitable ventilation. In this case, shredded paper will make the best bedding; there will be room to spread it and it is hygienic, as it can be changed every day if necessary and destroyed afterwards.

Another alternative for outdoor accommodation may be the garage or tool shed; either of these will save the considerable expense of a separate kennel and at the same time be just as comfortable, though, of course, the addition of an outside run is

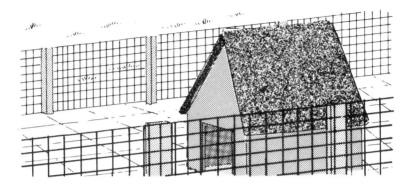

necessary, if the dog is not free to roam the garden or house during the day. I have seen a very good garage conversion into small-part-kennel by simply cutting a small hatch with covering door to close at night in one of the front double doors of the garage. When the dog is inside at night he has considerable freedom and a comfortable basket tucked in one corner. The tool shed can, of course, be used in much the same way.

From the point of view of guarding the house, the dog is really in a much better position outside for detecting a suspect on the prowl. I have read about a number of big country houses being burgled, with two dogs on the premises that have heard nothing. This can well be understood if they were located in the distant kitchen and as far removed as possible from any of the bedrooms, where entry is normally made. This sort of thing makes very bad reading, as the vast majority of dogs will make a great fuss at night if there is any unusual disturbance.

It is for you to decide which is the best accommodation for your particular circumstances, and I hope these few points I have raised will be of some help to you.

When you bring the puppy home and are deciding where he shall sleep, you will probably not have overlooked the fact that he will need a few items of equipment, one or two of which are essential to his well-being. The wardrobe is not very extensive, unless he is one of those smart town dogs that need that little extra. This reminds me of the lady I met some years ago who had just bought an expensive twin pram from a West End store for the sole purpose of transporting her two Pomeranians from a spot in Mayfair into Hyde Park each day. Believe it or not, this is quite true and, to say the least of it, this is spoiling in the worst possible form.

To return to the puppy again, your first thoughts will be of a collar and lead or harness. Let me say at the outset that none of these is immediately necessary if the pup is only eight weeks old; there will be time enough after he has settled down for a couple of weeks. In any case, I do not recommend his going into the street during this time if you have a garden or a suitable piece of open ground nearby. He is only a tiny puppy whatever breed he is and will not run very far at this stage. A very young puppy loves company and you may rest assured he will not wander very far from you or other human society. At three months or thereabouts, buy a leather collar, as light as possible in weight so as not to bother him too much, and a matching lead. A fairly good set should be bought, as cheap leather is a poor investment and does not take kindly to the rain. However, whether or not you can afford it, do not buy a very expensive collar, as from the point of view of size it will have to be replaced after three or four months when the dog has outgrown it.

The puppy must have his own drinking and feeding dish. These two bowls should be made of either earthenware, metal or plastic, in other words, be easy to clean, and with no corners in them where stale food can lurk. There are, of course, all sorts of shapes and sizes manufactured, so be careful to choose one suitable for your dog. If he is a Cocker Spaniel, there is a special bowl made for him which is small at the top, allowing just enough space for his mouth, but ensuring that his ears hang outside. There is another advantage about this type of dish in that it cannot be knocked over easily.

These, then, are the few essentials required for your puppy or dog to start with. It may be thought necessary with a young puppy in certain cases to use a dog coat in bad weather. Bearing in mind that the dog is quite a hardy animal, I do not recommend the regular use of a coat, though there are exceptional cases, such as convalescence, continual wet weather and so on. Normally a dog coat is used for warmth, but there is a very suitable waterproof coat on the market, which I have seen used to protect poodle coats from the wet. This is quite a good idea and can save a great deal of drying and grooming. If you do have occasion to use a dog coat, make quite sure it is well-fitting, particularly underneath and over the chest of the dog.

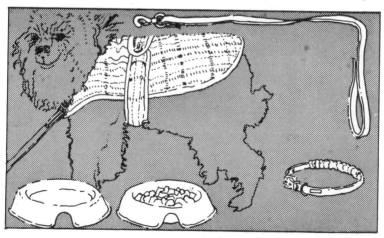

The brush and comb are items that will not be used a great deal on a very young puppy; nevertheless they will be very necessary when he is three or four months old. The average dog gets nothing like enough grooming, and I suggest five minutes every day will save a host of time and trouble at more irregular intervals. The comb itself should be made of steel and the teeth set coarse or fine according to the nature of the dog's coat. These combs are made with or without handles, and a good one will give life service. Dog brushes are also very varied. A dog with a short coat will need a hard, short bristle. The longer, silky coat will call for a handle brush with wire bristles set in a rubber pad; this type is very thorough in its work and does not tear the coat in any way, and it is easy to clear of loose hair. You will be well advised to get information from the breeder of the puppy on this point, or from your nearest pet shop.

An item you will have much less use for is the stripping knife, which professionals use for thinning the coat. Unless, of course, you are expert or are learning the art of stripping dogs, this can be a dangerous tool in the hands of a novice, particularly as some of the most efficient strippers have a razor blade incorporated in them.

For the dog's amusement, a rubber ball or bone are the usual items acquired, but having spent money on something like this you will probably find he much prefers the old slipper tied to his basket. Never give a chop bone, as this splinters and may choke or otherwise injure the puppy.

I think we have now catered for his necessary belongings, certainly for all that is needed to make him comfortable.

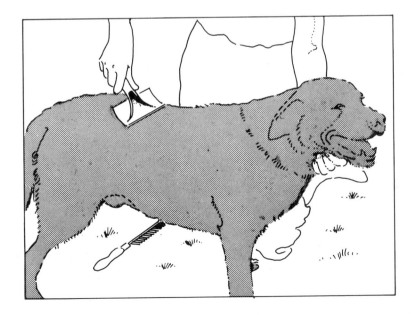

Puppy rearing

In an earlier chapter we have dealt fairly thoroughly with the question of choice of a puppy and we can assume you have made your decision and will need to know something about him, his care in rearing, feeding and general maintenance. Puppies are very much like babies, just eating, sleeping and playing; but before they do all these things they have to spend most of their first two months with the mother, strictly in her care. The tiny puppy will certainly need nothing more than the mother's milk to feed it for the first four weeks; and providing she is well cared for and gets ample nourishment, the puppy will have all it needs. It will hardly have seen the world at this stage and will just eat and sleep with the rest of the litter.

At four to six weeks, depending on its development, the puppy will start to lap milk with perhaps a few crumbs of brown bread soaked in it, and will advance day by day until at two months it will be quite able to leave the mother and stand on its own feet.

At eight weeks of age, it will need very careful feeding at intervals of every three hours (four or five feeds), and milk must play a very big part in the diet; solid food may certainly be introduced gradually, and perhaps one of the first solids may be a little milky porridge early in the morning. During the later morning, a small composite meal of cooked fish or meat scraps with a little grated vegetable may be fed, to which is added a cereal or a little dry brown bread broken into small pieces; the whole may be made appetising by the addition of a little gravy.

Although quantities are very important, it is impossible to lay down hard and fast rules on the subject, and probably the best guide is the advance of the puppy. It is certainly safer to under-feed than to give too much. The size and breed of the dog has of course, a bearing; but in dealing with, let us say, one of the terrier family, I suggest a meal of saucer capacity, not too full, amounting perhaps to 85 to 113 grams (3 to 4 oz) of food. His next two (or perhaps three) meals may be similar, but with any slight variation, such as fish for meat, or just cereal and gravy. His concluding snack for the day should again be milk, and given with time enough left for him to go into the garden and commence house-training.

It is a common fault to over-feed puppies, and I do suggest that the best advice should come from the breeder from whom you acquire the puppy, who should be happy to advise as to what the puppy has been used to having to eat. A lot of trouble can be started by giving a puppy just anything he will eat, regardless of whether he can digest it at this stage, so do try to take some trouble at the beginning, and you may be sure it will pay good dividends.

The average puppy in good health will bolt his food readily and would seem to have an endless capacity, but do not give second helpings. If by any chance he is not eager for food, it should be taken away until the next mealtime. It is a very bad thing to leave cold and stale food lying about for the puppy to eat when he feels like it.

It is usual at twelve weeks to stabilise feeding at four meals, but this must depend very much on the development of the puppy. At sixteen weeks, if the puppy has done well, a further reduction to three meals a day should be adequate. This process of elimination continues until at a year of age one good, well-balanced meal a day is sufficient for most breeds. The introduction of hard biscuit, either small or large, is advised at sixteen weeks of age, when it will be a great aid to the replacement of the baby teeth.

Further advice on this subject is given in the chapter 'Feeding' on page 28.

Nearly all puppies between eight and sixteen weeks will need worming if this has not already been done by the breeder. There is always a possibility of its being necessary a second time. Various proprietary medicines specially for this purpose are on the market. I always prefer to give a liquid rather than a capsule or tablet, which is more difficult to administer.

You may ask, 'How am I to know that the puppy is suffering from worms?' There are a number of symptoms that clearly indicate this. For one thing, more often than not there will be worms in the droppings. The puppy may have the unpleasant habit of scavenging or he may show a clear indication of looking very pinched at the loins or suffering a bout of diarrhoea.

If you are in any way uncertain, you can do no better than get in touch with the breeder of the puppy. It is seldom necessary to call in a veterinary surgeon for this minor trouble.

It has to be remembered that a dog must have a licence after six months of age, unless he is a working sheep dog or guide dog. This licence is obtainable from the Post Office. (See 'How much it costs', page 47.)

Puppy training

At this stage, we have dealt fairly thoroughly with the puppy's early behaviour, accommodation and feeding; but the very important matter of complete training must be continuous even at this early age. The dog that has been bred out of doors and kennelled there for a few months will naturally take a little longer to house-train.

The most sensible attitude is to compare a young puppy to a young child; they have a very great deal in common, a fact which should always be borne in mind. A child is reprimanded for any inexcusable misbehaviour, and the puppy must be treated in the same way.

At the outset, the puppy must have a permanent bed, which, as I have said, is usually located in the kitchen, and should take the form of a raised basket or collapsible bed. The latter should be raised well clear of the floor, so that it is free from draughts. The puppy must not be allowed to roam the house during the first few weeks; and provided he is allowed out of doors at frequent intervals, particularly after meals, last thing at night, and first thing in the morning, 'cleaning up' in the kitchen for the first week should be kept to a minimum.

It is a mistake to rub the puppy's nose in the offending puddle, but it certainly should be shown to him with the appropriate scolding. It is really surprising how well puppies know when they are at fault, and the typical reaction is a most guilty look, with the tail well down between the legs, and a very hasty departure into the corner of the room or behind the nearest chair. I have never found the employment of newspaper on the floor satisfactory, and naturally, if a puppy is encouraged to take advantage of this facility, he will get used to it, and consequently be under the impression he is expected to perform indoors rather than outside. I am quite convinced that the real answer to house-training is very regular habits during the early weeks, and – probably most important of all – you must give the puppy abundant praise when he is on good behaviour.

As the above suggestions are based upon many years of practical experience with young dogs in the home, I think we can safely set out the following points in order of practice, as being of prime importance:
1   Regular feeding.
2   Regular exercise.
3   Praise.
4   Mild punishment.
5   Patience.

Obedience training is something that is well within the scope of all dog owners, and there is no great secrecy about it. The subject is considerably simplified if one starts really early, in other words, from about three months onwards. What exactly do we mean by obedience training, or what can we reasonably expect from the puppy or dog? Well, I think for everyday needs and to convert him into something to be proud of and a credit to you, I would suggest he should come instantly to your call, walk correctly at heel both on and off the lead, and sit or lie flat upon command.

Party tricks and advanced training are generally speaking not necessary, although the average dog, with his high intelligence, will, upon reaching a reasonable standard of obedience, show a natural aptitude for additional accomplishments. A dog I knew quite well would, at the daily appointed feeding-hour, walk round the kitchen with his dish in his mouth as a gentle reminder that he was ready to eat. The same little fellow had occasion to move house, together with the family, to a new address some 80 kilometres (50 miles) away. The day after arrival he decided to return to his original address, which he proceeded to do on foot, and was found some twenty hours later sitting on the doorstep. Actions such as these seem inexplicable, but do go to prove that the dog has intelligence, and also a sense of direction that is lacking in civilised man.

It is a great mistake to allow too many people to make a fuss of your dog: he must know one master or mistress when it comes to training, exercise and feeding; and if more than one member of the family contribute towards his well-being in any of the above matters, exactly the same procedure must be employed, such as words of command, feeding-times, and so on.

It is safe to say that no two puppies are identical in disposition and temperament: one will have a natural aptitude for learning the difference between right and wrong, and another will be obstinate, highly-strung or strong-willed.

Winning the confidence of the puppy is the first step. Gentle encouragement for fifteen minutes with a kind word is worth more than a week of harsh treatment. I have never found it necessary to employ the use of titbits in training, but rather substitute an abundance of praise and make a great fuss of the puppy.

A puppy should not be allowed in any area frequented by dogs until it has had a full course of vaccinations. The vet will usually want to start the vaccinations at about 12 weeks of age.

Choose an open space or common for the first few outings, and if the puppy is quite young do not introduce the lead at all, but just encourage him to follow your direction, which he will probably do quite readily providing there is no outside attraction. A good spot for this initial walking is a narrow footpath, well screened on each side, thereby naturally confining the puppy to a position behind you. A great number of experienced trainers do not believe in the use of a lead at all, but I am afraid I cannot agree with this entirely, as the matter very largely depends on circumstances. If you are near a crowded shopping area or living on a main road, it is safer for all parties concerned to use a lead.

In the first introduction to a lead, I suggest using a one-piece appliance in the form of what is known as a slip lead (a single strand of cord with a loop at one end). This article gives the puppy the minimum of discomfort, as opposed to a collar and lead or a harness. The latter is sometimes described as a brace or chest strap.

The first outing on the cord lead will undoubtedly try your patience more than a little, and one should be content if the puppy makes an effort to walk at all. Your constant dragging at the lead is useless; and upon the first lead outing he will probably insist on remaining stationary for long intervals. To oppose this I have found the use of a small rubber bone or ball held in front of him will promote constant movement, and contribute to taking his attention off the lead which, after all, is the only thing that is worrying him at this stage. I know only too well that these one or two first walks can be very trying, but you have the consolation of knowing that the average puppy is very quick to learn, and after a few days you will see a great improvement.

Another quite effective method of getting a puppy to walk steadily is to get a neighbour's or friend's dog out with you at the same time, and thus provide a constant interest for the puppy. In this case the adult dog must, of course, walk in front of the youngster.

Assuming that the puppy is now not more than four months of age, his walking must be perfected during the few coming weeks. His correct position at heel means that his nose must be kept very close to your left leg; the lead should always be carried in the left hand, leaving the right hand free for emergency and general use. When the puppy has been walking for a few metres correctly at heel and upon a slack lead, you should praise him and give him a few pats of encouragement. These little attentions convey a tremendous amount to the dog.

A considerable problem to many dog owners is: when do I know it is safe to let my dog off the lead for the first time during the course of training? I am afraid there is no hard and fast rule about this, but I would suggest the introduction is made only when you have the dog walking properly at heel on a lead, and he is obedient to your call. I recommend that one day, when you are out on open ground and away from crowds and other dogs, you drop the lead to the ground at your side, making no unusual movement in doing so, and above all not faltering in any way in your step. I have found this practice very effective if carried out correctly, and if it is repeated a few times one can confidently detach the lead permanently, and be sure the dog knows his rightful position at your side. On no account forget the all-important praise during the course of these movements.

Half an hour or less is adequate time for actual instructions, and if this is lengthened the dog will rapidly tire and show complete lack of interest.

When the puppy is approaching six months of age, attention should be given to the next step in his training, which is to learn to sit and lie on command. These, of course, are two quite separate movements, and require two audibly different words of command. The words 'Sit' and 'Down' are the correct ones to use, as both are short and lend themselves to emphatic pronunciation. It is to be noted that the same word of command must always be used for the same movement, and an order should not be repeated more than once, raising the voice a little on the second occasion.

To start with, it will be necessary to place the dog in the sitting or lying position while simultaneously repeating the word 'Sit' or 'Down'. As soon as he shows some signs of understanding what you require you should use the word of command only, and cease handling the dog. Please remember that the same word should always be used for the same action, and that the word of command should not be repeated more than once. Nothing but the actual word of command should be spoken during the lesson time. If the dog fails to obey both on command and on the first repetition, then go back to the beginning again by placing him in the required position and repeating the word. If you fail to do this it may mean that when he is trained he will need to be spoken to six or seven times before he obeys.

One satisfactory method I have found to teach a dog to sit and lie is the following. While walking at a smart pace with the dog to heel, stop abruptly, and immediately the dog stops give the command 'Sit' or 'Down', as the case may be. By all means give the dog a chance to correct a wrong move, and he should not be punished for anything but wilful disobedience. Punishment should always be administered at the time and place, and not afterwards. If a dog is unaware of what his reprimand is for, he will get scared and will be very difficult to train at all.

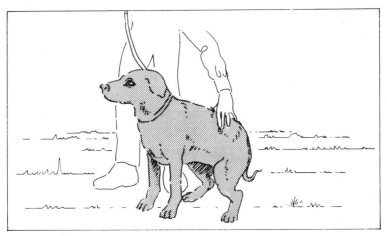

As yet I have made no comment on training the dog that has reached the adult stage, such as two or three years of age. A great number of people are under the impression that it is impossible to teach a dog very much at this stage of his life. This is definitely not so. A dog at, say, three years has certainly reached a very set way of living; but on the other hand his intelligence is fully developed, and this certainly makes him trainable, although the process may be a little more difficult. The same principles apply as are set out above, and nobody need hesitate to set about the task. This early training is really very simple in principle and based almost entirely on common sense and patience. Almost all dogs are able and willing to learn, and I am convinced that the high intelligence of our canine friends is frequently and grossly underestimated.

If your dog is of a sporting breed and you wish him trained for the gun he will still have to graduate through this elementary training procedure, and this is more than half way to his latter specialised training. You will be serving a most valuable purpose in his early training by inculcating the habit of obedience, upon which all his later and more complicated reactions will depend. In training for the gun I suggest you acquire one of the many excellent books on the subject. Training should be given between six and twelve months of age. You should, of course, in the first instance secure a great deal of useful advice from the breeder of your dog, who, being a specialist on the subject, should be able to help you into the right channels. Whatever dog you are fortunate enough to possess, his training is abundantly rewarded by many years of unfailing devotion.

The subject of keeping dogs with other pets is always arising and the clash, if any, usually involves our friend the cat. Many thousands of homes keep both a cat and a dog, and they are nearly always the best of friends, in spite of the fact that the cat is supposed to be the dog's natural enemy. In an emergency, a cat will 'hold its own' against a dog by adopting an aggressive attitude and depending upon claws for protection. But there is very seldom a real clash, and if any of you have any doubts about importing a young puppy into the home where the cat is firmly established, let me say at once there is no harm or risk involved, providing the introduction is gradual. Jealousy prevails among animals as with children and adults, and if there is friction between animals, in many cases this is the reason. See that all the family make a great fuss of the old-established pet while he is getting used to the new one.

The dog is by nature a friendly animal, and although he is the principle pet in the average home, he is not usually opposed to a little company other than human.

Children and dogs go together. In fact, broadly speaking, any animal is the source of a great deal of education to a child, to say nothing of the companionship between them. We read in the newspapers of children being bitten by dogs, and very unfortunately and quite wrongly this leads to a prejudice in the minds of some adults. These cases are the exception rather than the rule; you may rest assured that no animal will attack a child without a very good reason.

Frequently I have heard the remark, 'We could not consider having a German Shepherd Dog as we have young children'. There is absolutely no foundation for such a remark. In my opinion a two-year-old baby is too young for a young puppy, as damage will inevitably be caused on both sides: the baby will object to being scratched and knocked over, and the puppy will resent having his ears and tail pulled. When the child is four or five years of age and has some understanding of the difference between right and wrong, then is the time to have the puppy. The two youngsters will to a great extent grow up together and develop a thorough understanding. Naturally enough, my own children have grown up with dogs around them all the time, to say nothing of the rest of the farm stock, and I am sure they are quite fearless where animals are concerned. Strangely enough, the only creature that my small son was not on speaking terms with at the age of three was a snail.

Neither a child nor an adult should ever touch a strange dog. A friendly word, however, will certainly do no harm, and will help to gain the dog's confidence.

At this stage there is another subject that should be harnessed to children and dogs, and that is roads. This trio causes the authorities a very great deal of worry. The yearly casualties involving all three are enormous, and at the moment no real solution has been found in spite of education, dog-training classes, public lectures and so on. Let it be clearly understood that no dog, however well trained, should be allowed on main roads off the lead. There is positively no exception to this. If the ruling were rigidly adhered to, vast numbers of road accidents could be avoided, and this would be a great step in the right direction. It is comparatively easy to teach a child to understand, indeed a great deal has been done in this direction with success, but how can one blame a dog for running across a road without warning?

I am sure the average dog owner will endorse these sentiments, and already puts them into everyday practice; but there are still many who do not, and it is to those I would say, treat your dog as you would your child: there is not much trouble involved, and it will save many heartbreaks.

The dog's day

I think we can assume that the average dog's day is a very happy one, whether it involves sleeping on somebody's lap or racing after a dummy rabbit on a track. Like us all he is a creature of habit. Usually the first member of the household down in the morning lets him out into the garden for his run, or better still takes him for a proper walk. Actually this is a good time of the day for his grooming, which is not a long job, taking five or ten minutes at the most, and for making sure his bedding has a good shake out. If it is a fine day and not too cold, the basket can be put outside in the open, and remain there during the day. A number of dogs get a breakfast snack in the form of a few dry biscuits or dish of porridge; in any case see that he gets a dish of fresh water first thing in the morning.

It is amazing how quickly a dog will get used to your daily routine and fit himself into it. Judging by the number of dogs seen out with their mistresses shopping, one can safely assume this is in one sense killing two birds with one stone and that a visit to the shops is a very good reason for giving the dog a good walk in the morning. Many pets know that putting on one's hat or coat means an outing, and great excitement follows. Many a dog will fetch his own lead off the coat rack on a given cue, and one fellow I used to know was always waiting on the front door mat ready with lead and shopping basket at the slightest hint of a walk.

There are a lot of conflicting opinions about exercise and how much is necessary for the dog's well-being. I doubt whether one can lay down any hard and fast rule on this subject, as the breed of dog has considerable bearing on it; for instance, the requirements of a Dachshund cannot be compared to those of a German Shepherd. Many owners of small breeds will seldom take their dog beyond the limitations of the garden and, in spite of this restriction, the dog will probably maintain perfect health, and there is the advantage here that this is a good precaution against disease. Personally, I think it is a little hard on the dog to be confined to the garden all the time, unless of course the garden is exceptionally large, or he belongs to one of the very small breeds.

The morning is probably the best time for grooming, perhaps after his walk, as there is always the likelihood of its being a wet day, in which case he will need some attention after being outdoors, though it is a waste of time to attempt to comb him when wet. The short-coated dog is not much trouble in these circumstances, but a Pekingese or Cocker Spaniel can be quite a problem on a wet day if allowed to roam about the house after an outing. The best answer is to keep an old but clean dog towel handy with which to dry off the worst of it, and in the case of rough-coated breeds to keep the coat short and easily manageable.

In the summer months these breeds will need stripping at least twice during the season, and this in my opinion is a good thing for more reasons than one; skin troubles can be easily located with a short coat, and there is less to get wet. A breed such as a Cocker Spaniel cannot be stripped in the true sense of the word, but he should be kept trimmed around the feet, leg feathers and ears, the latter especially needing attention.

Grooming is not the tedious affair that some people seem to think and, providing it is regular, ten minutes will usually suffice. We have occasion to strip a number of dogs throughout the year and one can always tell the dog that does not get regular attention – he is restless all the time and positively hates the process.

A common daily ritual with many thousands of dogs is a conditioner of some sort. Generally speaking I am opposed to this and it can become very much a habit, serving no useful purpose. A dog is very much like a human being in this respect, and one has only to stop and think of the millions spent on patent medicines each year. A healthy dog seldom needs a tonic providing his food and exercise are given every consideration. One of the few corrective remedies I have occasion to use in the course of a year is the odd dose of liquid paraffin, which I feel is a very good lubricant and a great help to a dog that as a tendency towards constipation. If at any time you are not satisfied with the condition of your dog, and you have a clear conscience as regards his maintenance, I advise a visit to your veterinary surgeon.

Feeding

When we talk of a balanced diet, it is first of all necessary to consider what sort of food a dog needs and why he needs it. Basically, a dog requires the same food as man, his digestive process is similar, although very much stronger; the amount of roughage a dog can digest is surprising. Food provides for three things under the headings of growth, energy and protection. To ensure that your selection of food supplies all three, you must be sure what particular food is required for each. Fortunately for us, the dog can exist upon all sorts of food. I say exist, because the wrong diet over a long period is bound to have an effect that will in due course show itself in some form or another. To enable him to enjoy life to the full and be the minimum of trouble to man, it is therefore essential that he has sufficient food of the right kind.

At this stage, let us deal separately with our three headings outlined above. Growth depends on protein, and man's chief natural source of protein, throughout his history, appears to have been meat. We can safely say that meat in some form or another is necessary to our friend the dog.

Energy is derived from carbohydrates and fats, household scraps, vegetables, cereals and good quality biscuits. Scraps normally contain an ideal variety of carbohydrates, and consequently should not be wasted; fats are what the name signifies, whether they be of animal or vegetable origin.

Protection is given by vitamins and minerals, which are the invisible necessities of any diet. These necessary and indispensable food values have always been included in our own and our animals' diet, long before balanced diets were ever discussed or appreciated. The thing we have to find the answer to is in what form are the minerals and vitamins to be included in the diet. Over-cooking or stale vegetables will tend to lower the vitamin content of a diet. Meat in itself is not a complete food, and even in the times of the Stone Age the dog did not subsist on this alone, but in consuming the heart and liver of his prey obtained a proportion of these necessary items, the meat being balanced by the offal.

To provide your dog with growth, energy and protection you have thus to decide which three items of food will meet the requirements we have proved necessary, and I think the answer will be based on meat, biscuits and scraps. Meat can be obtained in several forms, including tinned; biscuit or cereal does not present any great problem and can always be substituted with wholemeal bread, which is preferable in stale or dry form. Vitamins and minerals will be found in our scraps, vegetables and tinned dog food in adequate supply.

It is very important that a dog should not get a monotonous diet. It is not difficult to get a little variation into his food; even if it means gravy one day and not the next, it is a change. Fish is quite a good item for one or two meals per week, and it is not necessary to go out and buy the best fillets; fish offal is quite good as long as it is well cooked. Potato in substantial quantities is not to be recommended, and from my experience most people realise this in feeding their dogs.

It is desirable that every dog should have something to chew on occasionally, such as a rubber bone or dog biscuit, as this is good for the teeth and the jaw. Bones can be dangerous because if they splinter, they can damage the dog internally. Rabbit and chicken bones should never be given to a dog.

Dog owners have often asked, 'Why does he pick up and chew stones?' This is probably because of the need for a bone or a toy to chew on, and this point should be watched, as stones are bad for the teeth and there is always the chance of his swallowing the smaller ones. I remember a Scottish Terrier I owned some years ago, who made a point of eating beach pebbles whenever she had the chance, until one day I found she could hardly move around for the weight she was carrying. After the operation, the veterinary surgeon showed me some fourteen medium-sized stones she had swallowed. I am glad to say she recovered and was cured of the habit.

There is no hard and fast rule for the number of meals required by an adult dog per day. From considerable experience I find the average healthy dog is quite happy on one good feed, and at most in addition perhaps a light snack of some dry biscuits in the morning. A dog over six months but under twelve months of age will, I suggest, require two medium feeds per day. From four to six months he will need three meals, and from two to four months four or five meals a day.

As with human beings, it is inadvisable to feed a dog before exercise or immediately after, and I have always made a point of

feeding my own dogs late in the afternoon, when any violent exercise for the day is finished, and yet there is time for the meal to be digested and for the dog to have a last short run. Water should always be available; but here again, do not let the dog drink unlimited quantities after heavy exercise.

If an attractive meal has been placed before him and for some reason he does not immediately take it, do not make the mistake of leaving it down for half an hour for his convenience; it should be taken up within five minutes and the dog not fed until the next mealtime. This may sound rather harsh treatment, but I assure you it is the correct attitude. If he leaves food untouched for some two or three days, it is then time to get a little worried and to call the vet. Serious loss of appetite is a symptom of many troubles, but in most cases an occasional loss of interest in food can be put down to perhaps lack of exercise, hot weather, shock and so on.

A common problem for new dog owners is quantity of food; here I would give a general answer at the outset and save worry. Let the dog be the best judge. By this I do not mean just feed him unlimited quantities, but study his general condition, weight, amount of exercise, and let these things contribute to the real answer.

Many people advising on dogs lay down specific weights for the solution, but I cannot agree with this entirely. As a general rule, while you are getting to know your dog and his needs, if you must err, it is safer to slightly under-feed rather than over-feed, and this particularly applies to young dogs.

I realise, however, that some sort of guidance is necessary, and I do not think one can go far wrong in suggesting 225 to 340 grams (½ to ¾ lb) of food overall for small dogs per day, 450 to 680 grams (1 to 1½ lb) for medium breeds, and between one and one and a half kilograms (2 and 3 lb) for the big fellows. There are, of course, exceptions to any rules. For example, a St Bernard may cheerfully eat and require nearly two kilograms (4 lb) of food per day. But it is certainly true that the dog owner should train himself or herself to have an idea of the weight of the dog's daily food, and keep to a reasonably consistent total weight for each day – largely in order to avoid the evils of over-feeding.

Travelling

The average dog compares very favourably to the human being in travelling by land, sea and air, and is often less trouble to take on a journey than a young child; for if he is with the owner all the time he has a certain confidence, which means that he will settle down at an early opportunity and accept the inevitable, as it were.

I have found from experience that quite a number of dogs do suffer from car sickness, however. In such cases travelling is miserable for both the animal and the owner. It is possible to administer a sedative for an individual journey but this is in no way a cure.

A dog will probably take more kindly to car travel if he has been introduced to it as a puppy, and has become what we may describe as gradually acclimatised to it. It is always a good thing to take the dog along with you if possible, as he will look after the car for you in your absence if he has been trained to it, and will be quite content to sit in a comfortable seat on guard for hours on end if necessary. Do remember, though, to leave a window slightly open so that he has plenty of fresh air, and in summer park the car in the shade. He should always travel in the back seat or in the luggage section of an estate car. Make sure that he is suitably tied by his lead, as tragic accidents have been known to occur through a car door opening and the dog suddenly jumping out under oncoming traffic.

I have on a number of occasions been asked to train a dog for car travel, and it is usually one that has not taken very kindly to it. While I am the first to admit that there is no definite cure, I have met with a fair measure of success by first allowing the dog to sit for some period on end in a stationary vehicle, and then taking him on very short journeys; in other words, introducing him gradually to the sensation of being in and travelling in a car. The best advice I can offer if you do constantly have trouble in this direction, and have tried remedies without success, is to leave him behind when your absence is of short duration; and if the journey concerns a holiday or any lengthy travel, consider alternative forms of transport, such as the railway.

An important point that is sometimes overlooked is the need to avoid giving the dog a feed before a journey. If he has to take a long journey, he can be fed on the way, when he is a little accustomed to the experience of travelling. The fact that to many dogs even a short journey by car is the cause of much excitement, apart from their reaction to travelling in the car, makes it inadvisable to give a feed just before setting out. Keep a large old raincoat in the back of the car, which can minimise both the effects of sickness and your own anxiety about it, which latter can have a bad effect on the dog.

If you do travel on public transport with your dog, I suggest that you not only consider the animal, but also your fellow-travellers, and thereby help to keep your dog the popular fellow he is with most people. There is nothing more annoying than seeing a dog in a railway carriage or on a bus making a thorough nuisance of itself by jumping over everyone in sight and climbing on the seats. This is definitely not necessary and certainly makes it very bad for other people travelling with pets.

If your dog is at all of a nervous disposition, do pick him up in your arms when getting on or off a public vehicle. There is no good purpose served by insisting that a nervous animal should board the vehicle himself. This is an occasion for avoiding trouble, and minimising the dog's fear of the unusual experience by carrying him. The dog should, of course, always be on the lead in a public vehicle, however obedient and reliable you know him to be.

When you travel with your dog on the bus, the admission of the dog is entirely at the discretion of the conductor, so both you and the dog should play your part in keeping his presence unobtrusive. My personal experience is that permission is not often refused, though I am myself opposed to the individual who tries to take a very large dog onto a crowded bus; this is not reasonable. In any case, all dogs must travel on the top deck of a double-decker bus, and this is one form of transport that many dogs do not enjoy. As I have suggested, carry him onto the bus if necessary, keep him under strict control but give him plenty of reassurance.

If a dog is travelling with you by rail, his admission is again at the discretion of the guard, but I have always found our railway officials extremely good with animals, and on many occasions they have gone to great and even unnecessary trouble to ensure their comfort. Generally the dog will travel in the coach with you, on payment of the child's fare, provided he is under proper control.

If you have to send your dog across country, then you will have to locate a specialist firm as most road transport companies do not cater for live animals. The dog must be in a suitable crate so that he has room to stand up and turn round if he wants to. He should also have a blanket to lie on and ample fresh air. In the absence of a costly hamper I have often received small dogs, and particularly puppies, in a converted tea-chest, which is admirably suited for the purpose, and is both strong and light in weight.

If you are the sender or recipient of a dog travelling alone, do ensure that he is met on time at his destination, and does not have unnecessary delay waiting to be collected. This can be an unnerving experience for an animal and should be avoided if possible.

Apart from the more common forms of transport, mention must be made of shipping and air travel. In the case of the former and upon the assumption that you are taking your dog abroad with you, there are some formalities required by both the Government and shipping companies. The shipping company will want to know all about the animal, primarily for the purposes of charges and accommodation. In the case of some of our larger ocean-going liners, canine accommodation is available on board, and it usually falls the lot of the ship's butcher to feed the dog, and generally ensure his welfare while on board. The shipping company will give you all the necessary forms, and will be pleased to advise you on quarantine regulations and so on.

Air travel for a dog may be regarded as something of a luxury, although many owners do avail themselves of it, particularly breeders who have made sales and are sending the purchase overseas in the minimum of time and with the minimum of trouble. You can transport your dog by air whether you are travelling with him or not.

Quite rightly, loose dogs are not allowed on aeroplanes: they must be dispatched in a container. The airlines will give you details of the type of box required, and will also specify the condition the dog must be in when received at the airport. There are a number of forms to complete when booking the flight, and the airline will need to know who is to collect the dog at the destination, if it is travelling alone. They will also give you all the necessary quarantine information. Costs are based on weight or volume plus a range of surcharges depending on destination.

The dog will travel in a specially set-aside section of the aeroplane. On a long trip, the dog would not necessary be confined in his container throughout the journey. The normal airline will, if instructed, exercise the dog at appointed stops, and generally speaking he is assured a most comfortable and effortless journey. Perhaps the only detrimental feature in this splendid form of transportation is the cost, but of course the additional cost involved is offset by the enormous saving in time.

Although perhaps few readers will find it necessary to have use for much of this information, the facilities are not commonly known, and if the occasion arises I hope it will prove of use and save unnecessary time and trouble.

Illnesses

A healthy dog is a happy dog: in fact this is true of all animals and human beings. The dog is very quick to show if he is off colour or really ill; and though like a baby he is unable to tell us what is wrong or how he feels, there are always certain unmistakable symptoms which either the owner or the experienced vet can detect, very often without difficulty.

The average dog should not suffer a lot of ailments. He was healthy to begin with and, if he has been raised on the lines laid down by authority and experience, beyond minor troubles one can safely say he should lead a happy and healthy life to an average age of twelve or fourteen years.

His being a hardy animal does not mean that we can neglect certain precautions in his maintenance, and there are several forms of particularly virulant diseases to which he is exposed, and which are common only to dogs.

Cleanliness is all-important, whether it takes the form of keeping the dog himself clean, his bedding, or his feeding bowls. It is incredible how much trouble starts from this source and one cannot take too much trouble. How many of us take the trouble to clean a collar and lead once in a while or scrub out the basket several times during the year? Prevention is certainly better than cure. Inevitably a certain amount of trouble is picked up in the streets, and I always suggest that a young puppy should not go out from his own domain (providing, of course, a garden is available) until he is a few months old or after he has been inoculated. He is going to suffer no hardship through this and will certainly be safer for it.

It is very unwise to let any of your friends fondle your dog if they have an infected animal or have been in contact with one. Any dog which is a suspect must be isolated in any case. From my experience the principal sources from which troubles are brought to dogs are the streets (even brought in by human beings) and any place where dogs are congregated.

As with human ailments, many serious complaints start from the common cold or chill, and a dog that has been out in the wet should be rubbed down on returning home, and care taken that he is not allowed to sleep in a draught. This applies particularly to domestic dogs, which are perhaps not quite as resilient as the sporting varieties that enjoy the freedom of the country all day.

In dealing with colds, the usual symptoms are shivering and some slight discharge from the eyes or nose; the appetite may not be affected in the early stages. In any case take the dog's temperature and satisfy yourself his fever is not too bad. Treatment is very simple: warmth is all important, and a mild laxative is a good thing, given on an empty stomach. Do not give the dog cold food for a few days, but see that the chill is taken off.

Neglect of a cold may lead to bronchitis, which is a more serious matter, particularly if the animal is older. A cough or choking sensation is present with this, and possibly a wheeziness when breathing and asleep. A dog with a tendency to fat is the worst patient, and this should be reduced if possible by dieting. Simple treatment is best, and the dog must be kept in a warm room and at a constant temperature, and if he is one of the small breeds keep him encased in a woolly coat which well covers the chest and stomach. In no circumstances should he be allowed to get wet. The bowels should be kept in good order and if the dog is usually normal in this respect, an odd dose of liquid paraffin will be the best answer. If you are not satisfied with his condition in any way, call in your local vet, as I would recommend in all cases where there is any element of doubt.

Constipation is one of the most common of all minor ailments, and is usually a sign of the wrong food or not enough exercise. Immediately it is noticed, a mild laxative should be given in the form of liquid paraffin, or in the case of young dogs and puppies a teaspoonful of warm salad oil. From my experience, I have not found caster oil satisfactory.

Diarrhoea, particularly in puppies, I view with more concern, as it is often the forerunner of something more serious, and it must be eliminated immediately. One of the most common causes in puppies is the wrong food; in older dogs, meat that is inclined to be 'high' will show itself in this way. A light diet should be fed warm, and in the case of adult dogs preceded by a purgative.

Gastro-enteritis frequently follows the symptoms of diarrhoea, particularly in young dogs, and should be treated by a veterinary surgeon. This takes the form of inflammation of the intestines and may be caused by a chill or incorrect diet. One can determine the complaint by the fact that a thin and greenish excreta is passed and the patient will be found to strain considerably and suffer some pain. Food must be liquid and warm; milk or barley water should alleviate the diarrhoea, and this should be followed by a diet of light puppy food, as advised by the vet. The dog will not necessarily appear listless, but may be disinterested in food of all kinds. As already stated, qualified opinion is essential.

Parvo virus is another serious problem which has arisen in recent years, and the symptoms are similar to gastro-enteritis. Speak to your vet about having your puppy vaccinated against this when he is about twelve weeks old, as this is almost always fatal.

Another very serious complaint from which a dog can suffer is distemper. This disease is quite the scourge of the dog world and can, and often has, ruined a kennel of dogs. Enormous sums of money have been spent to fight the complaint, and thanks to modern science a tremendous advance has been made. I doubt whether in any disease has the value of prevention been better demonstrated than in distemper. Its parallel in the human field is possibly influenza or pneumonia. The vaccine and virus preventives can be administered only by a qualified man, and their value, in my opinion, cannot be disputed. In the dog world, there still appear to be two fields of thought as to the value of inoculation, and I can never understand why. This worthwhile precaution is not costly and I have seen much distress through dog owners listening to wrong advice; after all, we have to place ourselves unreservedly in the hands of the doctor, so why not the dog? Dog distemper is a disease caused by a virus, and is not recurrent.

The dog is most vulnerable up to the age of two years, although it will attack older dogs. The basic symptoms are as follows: lassitude, loss of appetite, sneezing, a cough and discharge from the eyes and nose; the dog will lose weight and there is a considerable fever present. He may be sick for about a month, but recovery has been made in half this time, where the attack has taken a milder form.

As always the dog must be kept warm, and well covered, and at the most critical stage nursed day and night. If the necessary nursing cannot be given, the dog should be sent away to an infirmary, for it needs every attention. Liquid or semi-liquid foods must be given: in fact anything which, included in a nursing diet, will tempt the appetite. Distemper is a highly contagious disease, and it is essential to take every precaution to isolate your dog, not only from other dogs but from dog owners as well.

While we have not the enormous space that would be needed to describe all canine ailments and their treatment, this chapter would not be complete without some mention of skin troubles, which commonly come under the heading of eczema and mange. These, though external complaints, are promoted to a great extent by internal disorders, and generally speaking are rather more simple to treat than many general diseases.

Eczema is set up by a condition of the blood, due to bad feeding or inadequate food; internal parasites will also on occasion be found to be the cause. To start with, cleanse the blood stream by giving a laxative or a good worm remedy which will help to this end. All artificial food should be withdrawn, and a meat diet substituted. The actual sores should be treated with boracic powder; but even better than this, use a prescription from your veterinary surgeon. Eczema is quite curable providing cleanliness is the main theme in everything. It is not contagious.

Mange is the more serious skin condition and can show itself in two forms, namely sarcoptic and follicular, the latter being the worse form. In the case of sarcoptic mange, the hair at the infected parts will fall out and areas of red broken skin appear. In both forms mites are responsible for the condition and are found in the hair and glands of the affected parts.

To begin treatment for sarcoptic mange, remove the hair around the affected parts so that they can be easily treated; and before applying a specific remedy, a warm bath, to which sulphur crystals have been added, should be given and the dog well dried. A prescription should be obtained from your vet for application to the affected parts, and these should be cured after some two weeks' application.

Follicular mange will need a great deal more perseverance and a veterinary surgeon should always be called in. In this case, rather than treat the affected parts only, deal with the dog as a whole, as the complaint spreads very rapidly and in view of the highly contagious nature of the disease one is never certain that a cure is completely affected. At the favourable season of the year, I am a great advocate of baths, the only treatment by which you are certain to reach every part of the dog.

In either case of mange, ensure that any infected bedding or blankets are thoroughly fumigated, or better still destroyed.

You may ask why the subject of worms has not been discussed here. This is because it is normally only puppies that suffer from this disorder, and it has therefore been discussed in the chapter 'Rearing a puppy'.

Boarding kennels

There may be a time when you will need to use a boarding kennels and this chapter should give you some idea of what to look for.

The kennel that is in its own class apart is that providing quarantine, where every dog and indeed most other animals must go immediately on coming into the United Kingdom. This type of establishment is conducted under the close scrutiny of the Government for obvious reasons. The period of quarantine for a dog is six months, and during this time he must be segregated from all other animals; he is returned to the owner at the end of this period. Charges vary in accordance with the size of the dog, but you will find some guidelines on page 47. There are a number of quarantine kennels in this country, especially near ports and airports. If you find yourself bringing a dog into this country, the importation and kennel formalities are usually handled by the transporting company or by a major travel agent. If they do not have full facilities for organising this, they will certainly give you all the information you need.

Boarding is a subject that provides for endless discussion, and I propose here to give you a rough guide as to how boarding kennels function, what to look for and where to go. By many dog lovers they are looked upon as a necessary evil, but I think this is rather unfair, as such kennels are usually run by those who are dog lovers themselves, and believe me looking after other people's dogs is a great responsibility and constant source of worry.

Assuming you are going away on holiday or through sickness the dog cannot be left at home for some very good reason, you will have to board him at a kennel in the vicinity of your home. Boarding kennels are now licensed by Local Authorities, and as a result are better and safer now than in previous times. There are, of course, still some kennels which are better than others, so you will be well advised not to walk into the first kennel you see without some recommendation, either from your vet or from some other reputable source.

A number of people like to see where their dogs are to be kept during the holiday, and quite rightly so, but there are still many kennels that do not permit people to look over their premises. If you are faced with this and are in doubt, do not leave your dog.

One cannot expect a dog to be housed indoors and allowed to sleep in the bedroom when he is boarded, but he certainly is entitled to a clean, dry bed in a kennel of his own, quite separate from other dogs. He should have plenty to eat and drink, according to what he is accustomed to, and be taken out for exercise each day. I am not in great favour of outdoor runs if the dog can be taken for a separate walk each day; troubles can so easily be left in one given spot and passed on from one dog to another. I know concrete can be washed down, but this is impossible if many dogs have to use one big run during the same day. Where dogs are kept in any number, the kennels should obviously be cleaned every day with a liberal use of disinfectant; and if, by any unfortunate chance, trouble is located in any given spot, this must be isolated at once, and the whole kennel thoroughly scrubbed out.

While no responsibility can be accepted by a kennel for the occupant, every precaution must be taken, and it is a wise kennel manager who examines every dog upon arrival. In no circumstances should a dog under six months of age be accepted. Many dogs are inoculated as puppies, and this fact should be noted when a dog is accepted into the kennel. Most boarding kennels will not accept a dog for boarding without proof of vaccination or booster vaccination during the previous 12 months. A good boarding kennel will be under the supervision of a veterinary surgeon, and his word should be law.

A number of people get worried about the thought of their dog fretting in their absence. In actual fact this seldom happens, and it is often the case that the dog thoroughly enjoys the change, particularly if others are in view and he is in the country, which is, after all, the right place for a kennel. Many dogs will go off their food for a couple of days, and this is no unnatural feature. However good the food may be, it is different, and the dog quite naturally will wonder where he is. I have frequently seen a dog, the morning after he has been left at the kennel, most relucant to leave the kennel for a run. Following some fifteen minutes spent in gaining his confidence, however, he trots out quite happily on the lead, and returns with a healthy appetite. The third day he will give the appearance of having stayed with you for a month, and so it goes on. A very great attraction to me with dogs is that there are never two alike; but all of them will respond to the right treatment.

After visting a kennel one can always get an impression as to what the owners are like and whether they are dog lovers, and it does not need white tiles and cushions to give the right impression. I would say this to the reader – beware of leaving your dog where the fees are abnormally low. Ask for prices from several kennels so that you can compare them (there are some guidelines on page 47).

If you have occasion to leave your dog while you are away, be sure to leave your holiday address behind. There is always the remote chance of trouble, when the kennel will find it necessary to get in touch with you.

Breeding

The great question here is, are you breeding dogs as a hobby or for business? Circumstances may have to provide the answer when it comes to dog breeding, but from a very considerable personal experience, I can say with assurance that very few people indeed are lucky enough to be able to make dog breeding a profitable living. There are many good reasons for this, any of which you may learn from established breeders.

To give a fair picture to the reader, let us examine both points of view, and deal in the first instance with the business aspect. I have seen many people launch into the world of dogs with little or no experience, and quite seriously a vast number of them think (or rather thought) that it was only a question of keeping a few breeding bitches of a certain breed, and offering the maximum number of puppies to an eagerly expectant market for high prices. Needless to say, anyone embarking upon this basis would not last long.

Let us look at it intelligently, and assume that you want a supplement to the main family income, are fond of dogs and probably keep one or two, and have often toyed with the idea of breeding and possibly making a little money. Do not choose a certain breed because everyone seems to have them: use some initiative and, after some dog show visits and very careful deliberation, settle for a particular breed and stick to it rigidly. Probably your first step will be to acquire two good bitches out of show stock and from an utterly reliable breeder. You may have to pay a good price for them, but in any case one good breeder will gladly help another, and if your puppies are well bred this may help you in finding a reasonable outlet for the young stock.

With two good bitches I do not suggest a great rush to procure a stud dog. Many good ones will be available for reasonable fees, and there is no great hurry. After you have had one or two good litters you may find among them a dog puppy that will prove a very profitable specimen to other people if not yourself, and to have a small but regular income from stud fees is an addition to the project.

Here we have found a small additional income to the actual puppy sales: now what is the next step? Showing your dogs is essential, and the reason must be obvious. The dog show is probably your best medium for advertising; it should result in sales and in contacts with other breeders and exhibitors, keeping you up to date with the breed in question. In addition, of course, there is always the possibility of personal awards – the ultimate triumph.

This, then, sums up very briefly what is necessary if you are to start breeding for the reason I have outlined above and do not expect to make a fortune. You may well ask what about the cost of such a venture. I have made no mention of it, as it is a very elastic subject; but as a very rough guide and on the assumption you are interested in the best, the prices on page 47 should give you some idea. You will need to consider the cost of breeding bitches; equipment such as housing, leads and so on; and general expenses such as food, veterinary bills for inoculations, bedding and so on.

Most people who indulge in dog breeding for a hobby can afford to do so, although typical of such breeders is the woman whose husband is the main breadwinner and who wishes to have a profitable interest of her own. I think it quite reasonable to say that nearly half of the people breeding and exhibiting today fall into this category.

Specially trained dogs

It is thought that the dog's wild ancestor was probably domesticated by prehistoric man some seven or eight thousand years ago, as a companion and watch-dog. Later he was trained for hunting, retrieving game and generally helping to keep the family larder filled. By the New Stone Age, about four thousand years ago, the dog was already serving man as sheepdog and cattle-herd. Roman Britain, some two thousand years ago, was famous for its hunting dogs, which were an important export to the Continent.

Doubtless his readiness to respond to praise and affection, and his liking for a regular way of life, helped to establish the dog's close bond of companionship with man, and this, with his intelligence, has made it possible to train him in various working capacities.

There is an interesting history related to nearly all the well-known breeds, and in most cases the present shape and appearance was bred to and introduced originally for some useful purpose rather than mere whim.

The Pekingese is exceptional, in that it was his appearance that was important. It is thought that he was originally bred at the Chinese Imperial Court as the animal nearest in appearance to the lion, the symbol of Buddhism, which had reached China from India. Pekingese were bred at the Summer Palace at Peking, under the personal supervision of the Emperor, and only the highest Court officials were allowed to own them. After the sack of the Palace in 1860, however, five Pekingese were left behind and eventually brought to England. One of them was given to Queen Victoria, who was instrumental in popularising the breed in Britain.

The Borzoi, originally a hunting and carriage dog, was also adopted as an attractive pet by the nobles at the courts of the Russian tsars. The home country of the Poodle, occasionally called the 'French Poodle', is, in fact, Germany. During the seventeenth and eighteenth centuries he was used in France for the purpose of hunting waterfowl; and the various forms of his clipped coat were used originally, not only to facilitate his unhindered movement through water, but also as a means of identification, whereby the various owners could quickly distinguish their own dogs when out with a hunting party. Greyhounds were among the dog pets at the Imperial Court of pre-Revolution France. The Spaniel was a favourite with the Spanish nobility some centuries ago, for both his decorative and his working qualities, and was introduced into this country some time before the days of King Charles II.

It is interesting to trace, in our own art and literature, the part the dog has played in the lives of our ancestors, as companion, pet and worker. Special training has long been given by the sportsman, the shepherd, the gamekeeper and the poacher. Of these, the training that makes the most demands on the dog is that given by the shepherd. It may be of interest to note that the English, Welsh and Scottish sheepdogs have their counterpart in Central Europe, in the German Shepherd Dog, often known as the Alsatian, from the place-name Alsace.

All these breeds rank exceedingly high in intelligence, and are second to none in the working field. A dog that is entrusted with the security and indeed the lives of other livestock, large and small (for dogs guard cattle as well as sheep), must be a hundred per cent sound, mentally and physically, to act as man's representative – which is what these dogs are doing in their guard work, for they have to be trustworthy in the absence of man. It is a wonderful sight to see two dogs dispatched unattended for hours upon end for the purpose of recalling sheep stragglers from a mountainside, where they work almost entirely on their own initiative, with but an occasional call by whistle from the shepherd.

On a small scale, dogs were in the past used in Britain as draught animals, and even just a few years ago in Belgium, the Newfoundland-type breed could be seen drawing the baker's cart through the streets in some places. The husky is the best known, for he has no parallel for his use as a sledge dog.

Since the end of the nineteenth century man has begun to realise, more than ever before, the great potentialities of the dog in a working capacity. Today dogs are employed not only by the Forces and public services, but also by industry. The companion to the night-watchman, the heavy lorry driver or the policeman is now given a planned course of training, in some cases lasting up to three or four months, the dog being in the first case carefully selected at an age of about eight months, when it is possible to judge whether he has that extra high intelligence that is necessary if he is to respond to the calls that the training makes on him.

Though the countryside has its centuries-old tradition of training the working dog, it is only quite recently that the almost unlimited possibilities of employing highly trained dogs in other ways has been really appreciated. The great strides made in recent years have shown that it is not only sheep herding that he can be trained to be even more useful than a human colleague.

The Bloodhound's capacity for following a trail is well known, and has long been utilised to some degree. Other breeds also have similar qualities and can be trained for this work. The German Shepherd Dog has been trained to locate people buried as much as six metres (20 ft) below the surface, and other dogs of various breeds have shown that they can be particularly gifted in such exploits.

The trained guard dog of today is very different from the 'good house dog'; he is the trained specialist as compared with the amateur. Whether he is being used by the Forces to guard airfields, or by industry to patrol with the night-watchman, or by the police to track criminals, his training has to be specifically planned and the dog must be carefully selected.

This is a completely different thing from merely training a dog to be unintelligently and savagely suspicious of the stranger. German Shepherd guard dogs, for instance, are not trained to be savage in any way; indeed, the essence of its usefulness is that a guard dog must always be completely under the control of the handler. Evidence of this can be found with police dogs who will, on command from their handler, attack the wrist of a man firing a gun at them. It is essential, therefore, that the dog employed on this type of work must have only one handler – or certainly no more than two. In no circumstances must all and sundry have access to him or make a great fuss of him. He is trained to take food from one person only and to refuse all other offered.

Apart from being trained to hold down a suspicious stranger without savaging him, and giving companionship and added confidence to his human companion, the sense of smell of the guard dog is of value. For example, many German Shepherd Dogs employed in department stores to patrol with the night-watchman, can detect people hidden completely out of sight 45 metres (50 yds) away. The police also make full use of this quality in their dogs, and police dogs have been trained to sniff out drugs, bombs and firearms.

After the dog's preliminary training, dog and handler must, of course, be trained together. Most courses last some six to eight weeks, and for the last part of the time the dog remains with the one handler, being fed, exercised and trained by him under an instructor. In most cases there is nothing particularly complicated about training. The great thing is for the handler to gain the dog's confidence – indeed, there must be equal confidence on both sides.

But whether a dog is taking one of these newer courses or being trained for the gun or as a sheepdog, the basis of the training – and the part on which success is completely dependent – is exactly the same as that required by the dog being trained to be a pleasant companion in an ordinary household. The dog must learn obedience; and as we want him to use his intelligence and all his facilities fully in following commands, he must learn that obedience through his confidence in his trainer – not through fear.

All training is based on this which, when it is perfected, leaves the balance of any intensive training a straightforward matter. Retrieving and staying unattended in any one given spot, attacking and seeking, and other special training will be readily acquired by the dog who has confidence in the handler and has learned instant obedience to the simple basic words of command, which means that he has the habit of instant response and can distinguish one command from another. Not every dog has the capacity to learn more complicated duties, just as we cannot all be ballet dancers though the ballet dancer must share the common knowledge and discipline of walking. The degree of training given to the household dog companion will largely depend on the amount of trouble, patience and interest that the owners are prepared to give to it.

Even without specialised training almost every dog has great loyalty to his owners and will bark if he hears an intruder or senses unusual movement, especially at night. Fortunately for our community, the criminal does not like dogs of any kind, the fact that they can make a lot of noise being in itself a deterrent to his activities.

One great errand of mercy that falls to the lot of the dog is companionship for the blind. Dogs have been employed in this capacity for some years, and there are a number of fine training-schools solely designed for this purpose. A great variety of breeds are employed, but the most popular is the Yellow Labrador or a

Golden Retriever-Yellow Labrador cross. This fine work involves a considerable amount of training, which takes five to six months. Selection of the dogs is also a difficult matter, as the dog who is to do this work must have particularly acute sight and hearing and the highest possible degree of intelligence if he is fit to be responsible for his owner's safety crossing roads, negotiating stairways and following a normal way of life.

The blind applicant for a dog has to go to stay at the training school for three weeks, and is first introduced to the various dogs there. The choice of the dog for that particular person is made most carefully, and is largely dependent on the response of a particular dog to a particular person. In this work, of course, the need for equal confidence on both sides is particularly great.

The blind person and the dog are trained together during these final weeks. The basic requirements from the dog are the same as for all training, but must be supplemented by special work that can only be done by dogs with outstandingly high intelligence. An incredibly strong bond of understanding and affection develops between dog and owner; but the general public should remember that such a dog, especially when actually 'on the job', is a specialist at work, and they should never attempt to pet him or distract him from his job. Nobody would attempt to discuss the weather with an actor in the middle of a play or with a racing driver in the middle of a race; and we should equally respect the worker's need for concentration when we meet one of these trained dogs. There is no doubt that they know what they are doing and what they have to do, and they are a boon without parallel to their owners.

There is a long waiting list for these dogs, and our aim must be to see every sightless person in possession of one. Apart from its not being easy to find suitable dogs, it is a costly business (see page 47), a fact to remember when we see a box marked 'Guide Dogs for the Blind'.

How much it costs

Obviously the cost of buying and keeping a dog varies tremendously depending on the size and rarity of the dog, your own choice of the type of food and equipment, and so on, so these prices are merely designed to give you some rough guidelines on how much it will cost to keep a dog.

Before embarking on anything which may involve you in substantial expenditure, such as buying your first puppy or sending your dog to a kennels while you are on holiday, it is best to obtain a few quotations from kennels, breeders or other suitable sources in your area.

Baskets   Dog baskets and boxes start from about £5.

Boarding kennels   Kennel and quarantine kennel charges depend on the size of the dog. A standard Poodle, for example, would cost about £25 a week at a kennels.

Breeding bitches   Prices here vary from £100 to £1,000 as the price depends on age, pedigree and so on, but you should expect to pay at least £100.

Equipment   A collar and lead costs about £1–3. Feeding bowls cost about £1. A brush and comb costs about £5. A dog coat costs about £6.

Food   Fresh meat prices vary, but you will get the best price from your regular butcher. 400-gram tins of dog meat cost between 25p and 40p. 3-kg bags of dog meal cost between £1 and £1.50. 650-gram packets of dog biscuits cost about 80p to £1.

Guide dogs   It costs about £1,000 to train a guide dog for the blind.

Inoculation   A full course of inoculations for a puppy will cost upwards of £20.

Licence   The dog licence costs 37½p.

Puppies   An eight-week-old puppy of a reasonably common breed will cost between £85 and £120.

Major breeds

Popular small breeds include among others the terriers (except the Airedale), Pekingese, Welsh Corgis and spaniels. Apart from purely personal preference, the general advantages of the small dog are that he has an appreciably smaller appetite than the big fellow, and needs less exercise and house-room. He can easily hold his own when it comes to intelligence and character.

Among the large breeds we have the gun dogs, except the spaniels, the Airedale, Borzoi, Retrievers, Setters, Sheepdogs, except the Shetland, and, of course, the St Bernard. Apart from working, the large breeds are generally not suited to life in towns. Given facilities for feeding, accommodation and exercise, however, the big dogs can easily compete with their small cousins when it comes to affection and companionship, and are delightful with children.

Whatever you choose, small or large dog, thoroughbred or cross-bred, always look out particularly for a bright, alert puppy. He must have clear eyes, and no sign of rickets in his front legs (in other words, the legs should be straight if this is laid down for that breed). As has been said, you would be very wise, in any case, to secure a veterinary certificate of health when buying any puppy.

The symbols next to each illustration will give you an idea of whether the dog is very large, large, medium or small.

Afghan Hound
Illustration from Duphar's Kavak dog chart.

Termed a medium to big breed and now relatively common. The breed is registered at the Kennel Club with a separate classification and the grant of Challenge Certificates. Originally used as a hunting dog by the hill tribesmen of Afghanistan, and it is quite unique in appearance; the long silky coat extends to the feet, the legs having a 'baggy' appearance when covered with an abundance of hair; ears are well-feathered and pendulous; the face is narrow and smooth; the tail well-carried and curving at the tip. The breed is very graceful in appearance and but for the long coat is of greyhound build. It has a long head and dark eyes, is very graceful in movement and generally sedate by nature. Colours are fawn or red in most cases. This is a dog with a great history and an equally good house dog, but needing considerable attention to look his best. Height to the shoulder should be 69 to 74 cm (27 to 29 in), and the weight about 29 kg (64 lb). Bitches are about 5 cm (2 inches) smaller.

Airedale Terrier
Illustration from Duphar's Kavak dog chart.

The present Airedale Terrier originated in the valley of the River Aire in Yorkshire and is the result of a cross between a native hound and terrier. The breed is quite a powerful one although not very big.

The dog has every characteristic of a small terrier with a hard wiry coat, black and tan in colour, and needing stripping each year. He has small V-shaped ears, a square muzzle, back short and straight; likewise the legs are perfectly straight. He is a big-boned dog and stands strong and firm. He has small eyes and ears, with a thickset neck; a flat skull and long head with a deep and powerful jaw. The tail is usually docked in a puppy to about half its length. The breed weighs upwards of 18 kg (40 lb), some specimens reaching nearly double this weight. A dog can reach 61 cm (24 in) at the shoulder. Bitches are usually a little smaller. The Airedale is a natural guard dog, intelligent and alert, and a formidable adversary. The police forces have used these dogs with success. They are not born fighters as some people suppose, but will certainly hold their own in a scrap.

Basset Hound

Illustration from Duphar's Kavak dog chart.

This is very much a dog of character, and is quite in his own class. He has a long and powerful body with great depth through the ribs, the neck is thickset and strong. The head almost gives an appearance of being dome-shaped, which is probably accentuated by the long narrow face or snout; the brow and sides of cheeks are very wrinkled, the long ears are set low and should hang very evenly in folds; the eyes are deep set. The front legs, which are about 10 cm (4 in) long, fit closely together to the chest, incline inward from the elbow to the knee, and outward from there to the feet, which are turned outward and large. For a small dog he is quite muscular, and strong, his weight being about 25 kg (55 lb). His colour is hound marked, black, tan and white, or lemon and white. The coat is flat and smooth, and retains a fine polished appearance.

Beagle

Illustration from Duphar's Kavak dog chart.

These dogs have always enjoyed considerable popularity in their own field in the country, and on the show bench, but they are becoming more popular as pets. The Beagle is very old indeed and has been recognised for some centuries; although very much a hound in appearance, these smaller dogs in no way resemble the Foxhound. The head is powerful and dome-shaped, with long ears. The Beagle has fine, short hair, a deep chest and rather short body; the ribs are well sprung and the dog is very muscular. The forelegs are straight, and the feet round and well-padded for cross-country work. Colouring is hound marked in a variety of typical markings and the coat may be smooth or rough, the former being far more general. Dogs can grow to as much as 41 cm (16 in).

Bedlington Terrier

Illustration from Duphar's Kavak dog chart.

Another lesser-known breed, but gaining in popularity. The build is like that of the Whippet, but the coat is more like that of a Dandie Dinmont, to which breed the Bedlington is undoubtedly a cousin. The head and arched body are probably the most distinctive features. The muzzle is long and tapering and the head narrow, with almost a straight line from the dome to the tip of the nose. The body is moderate in length with flat, deep ribs. The ears are of medium size and lie flat on the cheeks. The silky topknot is not unlike the Dandie's. The coat as a whole is short and hard with a soft undercoat, and is very thick in texture. Acceptable colours are dark blue, sandy liver, blue and sandy tan. The dog stands at about 38 to 41 cm (15 to 16 in), weighing little over 9 kg (20 lb); the eyes are small and sunken. The breed, in my opinion, has a great future and it is up to the fanciers to see that it achieves the place it deserves in the dog world.

Bernese Mountain Dog

(See cover illustration)

The Bernese Mountain Dog was originally used as a cattle-herd by the Swiss farming communities, often helping to move the animals from their summer to their winter pastures. The farmers also used them to pull their farm carts to market. It is a medium size, strongly built dog with a long, wavy coat which is black with tan and white markings. The head is square and the eyes dark. Bernese Mountain Dogs are usually hard-working and of an even temperament.

Bloodhound

Illustration from Duphar's Kavak dog chart.

The breed is said to have been introduced into Britain during the Norman conquest, and legend is probably correct in this instance, for we know these dogs hail from France, where they were bred as sporting dogs, using the powerful scent for which they are so famous. The Bloodhound is one of the oldest of sporting breeds. He is a big dog, about 69 cm (27 in) tall and weighing around 50 kg (110 lb) and his rightful place is the country, where he is happiest. These dogs have been used with very great success for tracking, at which they are experts, and consequently many police forces have made good use of them from time to time in prison escapes and so on. A well-trained dog can well use a scent up to 24 hours old. Bloodhounds that have been trained are often used in pairs. Their most conspicuous feature is the great looseness of skin, particularly round the head and jowl. The ears are long and silky and set low. The eyes give the appearance of being bloodshot, which is not the case: it is due to the down-drag of the flews, which causes the inner skin of the lower lid to be shown. The back has a strong appearance and is long; the dog has heavy bone and a straight leg. This is a dignified dog and reputed to have a very even temperament. Breeding is now limited in Britain. This is very definitely a country-man's dog.

Border Terrier

This great little sporting breed will tackle anything in the vermin world. As indicated by his name, he hails from the Northumberland/Scotland border and is a great and established favourite there. He is not actually bred for killing, but rather for earthing foxes etc. The head gives the appearance of being square, its breadth being accentuated by a short muzzle. He usually has a short, hard, wheaten-coloured, or black and tan coat. He will run with the horse or hunt with the hounds and cover long distances each day. The recognised weight is 5.9 to 6.8 kg (13 to 15 lb), and he stands 33 to 41 cm (13 to 16 in) at the shoulder. Overall a popular terrier that is rapidly gaining in fame for his great sportsmanship; he fits in very well to the average home but of course is happiest in or near the country and is great for keeping rats under control. The Border is another breed not easily recognised on the street, but is to be found strongly represented at the big shows; he would be even more popular if better known.

Borzoi

Illustration from Duphar's Kavak dog chart.

It is fairly common knowledge that the Borzoi comes from Russia and was very popular at the courts of the tsars, where these dogs were kept in packs and used by the Russian nobility for hunting wolves. The breed has become widely dispersed since that time and today is probably not very much in evidence in its original native land. Perhaps it is rather drastic to suggest that this dog is just for beautiful ornamentation these days, but nevertheless it can be found only in very few homes, and of course at dog shows. Borzois really are handsome looking animals and among the biggest of breeds. They have the lines of a greyhound in almost every respect, and are conspicuous for their attractive coats and colouring. They are very fast, as they used to follow the horse, and strong in build. The coat is long and silky and inclined to curl; white, fawn and white, lemon and white are the most common colours. The head is very long and sleek, and really artistic in shape, ears are small and placed well back, chest is narrow and very deep, back well-arched, with very strong loins; front legs are straight. Upon examination the whole dog would appear to be very bony; to some extent this is so, but it ensures stamina rather than bulk weight, and incorporates perfect balance. Without doubt, the most aristocratic of all breeds, but owned by the very few. Average height (at shoulder) is 71 cm (28 in).

Boston Terrier
Illustration from Duphar's Kavak dog chart.

This American breed was first recognised over a century ago, and even now it has not attained in Britain the popularity it enjoys in the States. As the average dog owner may guess, the original cross was an English Bull Terrier with a Bulldog, and the results are, I think, a very even distribution of both features. The Boston Terrier is about the same height as a Fox Terrier. For many years this was America's most famous breed. He is a very compact little dog, weighing 6.8 to 9 kg (15 to 20 lb), and very easy to maintain. He closely resembles the French Bulldog. Few people can afford this breed in England, and importation is not easy. The ears are not cropped in the UK.

Boxer
Illustration from Duphar's Kavak dog chart.

Originally a German breed, the Boxer has been recognised for almost a century, and is now an extremely popular dog. The breeds which were used as foundation stock are unknown, although the Bulldog was certainly one of them. Bred as a guard dog, the Boxer is an energetic and active dog which demands a great deal of exercise. Its frame is muscular; weight about 30 kg (66 lb); height about 61 cm (24 in). The coat is fawn or brindle with white markings, and should be short and glossy. The distinctive feature of the Boxer is the foreshortened muzzle, broad jaw and black mask. This is a good natured dog, suitable for a family with plenty of room and plenty of energy. The ears are not cropped in the UK.

Bull Terrier

Illustration from Duphar's Kavak dog chart.

A very courageous and popular breed; a number of these dogs used to be susceptible to deafness, but this flaw has now diminished. The Bull Terrier was originally used for fighting and bull baiting during the eighteenth and nineteenth centuries, and may still be seen in old prints in the fighting-pits, for which in those days he was entirely bred. The modern dog has changed little, though in the show ring there are few breeds that show off so handsomely as this somewhat rugged fellow. He is not a big dog, and is very easy to maintain with his short cropped coat; average weight is about 21 kg (47 lb), and height about 56 cm (22 in). He is a good guard as well as companion, perfect with children, although not so appealing to look at as the Cocker Spaniel. He enjoys a big popularity in Britain and this is evenly distributed, being found as much in the north as the south. The Bull Terrier must definitely go on the short list of popular dogs.

Bulldog

Illustration from Duphar's Kavak dog chart.

One of the few breeds in Britain recognised upon sight by the entire populace; indeed it should be, for it is still one of our national emblems, and is accepted as such the world over. The Bulldog is not a big dog, but a very solid one in every respect; weighing about 23 kg (50 lb). He gets through life in his own time and, contrary to appearances, is one of the most docile of breeds and particularly good with children. If, of course, he does decide to get hold of anything, it needs more than hand effort to prise open the powerful jaws. The Bulldog is said to be a difficult whelper, and this may be a reason why there are only a limited number of good breeders in Britain; also there is the fact that he is rather an expensive purchase. His most outstanding feature is the head, which is wide and very wrinkled; the skull is flat and the ears set well up on the top; he has a large nose set right back between the eyes; the front legs are very short and strong, with a great width of chest, said to be comparable to that of a racehorse; the flanks are set high and sloping to the shoulder. The dog is very muscular but the general build does not make for easy movement, so he is less agile than other dogs of a similar size. It is safe to say his reputation makes him popular rather than his appearance and build. Colouring is varied and broken, a broken head marking being very attractive in this breed.

Cairn Terrier   Illustration from Duphar's Kavak dog chart.

One of our very popular small dogs with lots of spirit and an aristocrat in his own field. The Cairn is really a game little fellow and comparatively trouble-free as regards maintenance. He has a small, sharp, foxy head with prick ears; he carries his tail well up, with a compact little body; colouring varies but is more often than not grey brindle. There seems little doubt that he was the original Scottish Terrier, and that the latter as we know him today is the forerunner of the Cairn. He has a hard, wiry coat which does not require stripping, his body is very compact and on the short side. The average weight is 5.4 to 6.8 kg (12 to 15 lb), and the height about 25 cm (10 in). Knowing the Cairn, one can well understand his popularity in all walks of life. If one is not opposed to short-legged dogs, this breed well deserves consideration for the average home. Though likeable and friendly, he is a good guard dog, as he is alert and intelligent.

Chihuahua

Illustration from Duphar's Kavak dog chart.

This lively little dog is one of the smallest of the toy breeds, weighing only about 1.5 kg (3 lb). The coat can either be short and smooth, or long and soft with feathering on the feet and legs, a ruff on the neck and a plume on the tail. Colours vary, the most common being tan or tan and white. This neat pocket-size dog is ideal for people with a small amount of space. It makes a good companion for it is quick, alert and active. Despite its size, it can be a good guard dog as it will seldom remain quiet if it hears an unusual disturbance.

Chow-Chow

Illustration from Duphar's Kavak dog chart.

A dog unique in more respects than one: I should know (or, rather, should have known better!) for on the one and only occasion I have been nipped in handling many thousands of dogs, it was a Chow that left his mark. He was sitting on a show bench, minding his own business, and I should have been minding mine, and that is how it happened – but then I was very young. He is a very dignified dog, friendly when you know him, which is a good attitude for a dog looking after you and the home. He is very hardy and has the distinction of a black tongue. He weighs upwards of 18 kg (40 lb) and is of medium size, being about 46 cm (18 in) or more high. He has a lion-like appearance, with blunt features and a beautiful coat of red, black, yellow, blue or sometimes white. This is a breed where colour can have a marked effect on the price asked. He has a curled tail, carried well over his back.

Cocker Spaniel

Illustration from Duphar's Kavak dog chart.

The Cocker Spaniel is an extremely popular breed, which is easily understood; for it is a most appealing-looking dog, the right size, attractive and an excellent companion for both adults and children. He fits into the average home well in every way. Normally the owner does not spend enough time on the maintenance of the coat, which does need more attention than that of a short-coated dog. The Cocker Spaniel is one of quite a large family, which includes the English and Welsh Springer, the King Charles, the Field and the Clumber Spaniels, and unfortunately none of these has reached the popularity of the Cocker. He is a fairly small dog, weighing about 11 kg (25 lb) and the most common colourings are red, black and roan. He has a short back compared to his cousins, and is altogether fairly compact. The neck is long and muscular, and the shoulders sloping. The flanks are level with or rather lower than the back. The coat is flat and silky, and legs are well feathered. He has long ears, well covered in hair. These need particular attention when you are grooming. (See also cover illustration.)

Collie, Border

Illustration from Duphar's Kavak dog chart.

This working dog has been known for hundreds of years, but it got its name in the late nineteenth century when it was one of the most successful breeds in the early sheepdog trials on the England/ Scotland border. As with many working dogs, Border Collies were bred to produce good animals for the job of herding sheep, without

59

regard to breed standards. It is only recently, therefore, that they have been recognised by the Kennel Club. An attractive dog, usually black and white, with a long glossy coat with short hair on the face and legs. The head is broader and shorter than that of the Rough or Smooth Collie. The height should be about 53 cm (21 in). The dog is well-known internationally and is one of the best sheepdog breeds. It has been used as part of the breeding stock for the Australian Kelpie and the Australian Cattle Dog. The Border Collie is an energetic working dog and not suitable as a pet in most households.

Collie, Rough

Illustration from Duphar's Kavak dog chart.

The Collie is and always has been a very exclusive breed. It is a fairly large dog and very attractive. The two outstanding points of the breed are the head and coat. The head is of great length and very graceful in appearance. The thick long coat is in several shades of attractive colouring, including fawn and white, sable and white, and tricolour; the dog has a dense undercoat for protection. The skull is flat and tapers to the nose, with ears small and semi-erect, and brown almond-shaped eyes. The body is long with deep chest, and the body slightly arches to the loins. He is a fairly big dog and would not readily fit into every home. The height is about 61 cm (24 in). His coat, one of his outstanding features, needs a lot of attention to look its best; he is a devoted companion and second to none in loyalty to his master. He is extremely faithful, with a gentle temperament, is intelligent and is easy to train. He loves human company and requires a good deal of exercise.

The Smooth Collie carries the same points, the only marked difference being the coat, which is flat and rather hard in texture. Most common colours are sable and tricolour.

Dachshund, Smooth-Haired   Illustration from Duphar's Kavak dog chart.

Another dog of German origin which has found its way to Britain and nearly to the top of the tree in favour. The breed was originally introduced and made popular by Queen Victoria and Prince Albert; at that time this was still a sporting breed in Germany, although it has never been really used in this capacity in Britain. Dachshunds are, however, possessed of all the attributes of a sporting dog, as well as having a most attractive, appealing appearance. They have wonderful characters and are excellent house dogs, with a penetrating bark that can be used very effectively. It can be well understood why the Dachshund is so popular, as it is small, intelligent, compact and trouble-free, and costs little to maintain.

The average weight is in the region of 9 kg (20 lb) for a standard Dachshund; miniature breeds are also fairly popular. It has a long body with a deep chest. The short, smooth coat is usually red or black and tan in colour; the front legs are very short and the elbows well tucked in to the chest. The head has a sharp appearance and tapers to the nose. This is an excellent dog in every way to keep where space is limited, but he is also most happy in the country and can stand a great deal of exercise, though this is not absolutely necessary.

The Long-Haired Dachshund is a slightly lighter-weight breed, but the only real difference is in the long, silky, attractive coat lying close to the body, with leg and tail feathers. Altogether he is a most attractive and likeable little dog. In both Dachshunds the tail should be set on fairly high, and be strong and tapering, not too long or too much curved; and it should be carried so that it continues the line of the body.

Dalmatian   Illustration from Duphar's Kavak dog chart.

This breed, often known as 'plum pudding dogs' lost their vocation when people gave up their grand carriages, as it was thought fashionable in the nineteenth century to have a Dalmatian running alongside your carriage. Thanks to the efforts of a few exhibitors, however, they have become popular again. It is a mistake to suppose they are only suitable for stables: they are excellent guards, having a very deep voice; their coats are short and easily kept clean; and they behave very well domestically. They have similar body points to those found in all sporting breeds. The legs must be quite straight and the hind legs carry a lot of muscle; feet are round and hard, and consequently able to take a lot of exercise. The head is of moderate length, skull flat and broad between the ears; the ears are of moderate size and carried high. Markings are important, particularly in show dogs: the spots should be round and clear and distinct from one another. This breed will make a good guard dog, and is found in considerable numbers in the modern home where they make great companions. The maximum height for a Dalmatian is 61 cm (24 in) and the weight about 24 kg (53 lb).

Dandie Dinmont   Illustration from Duphar's Kavak dog chart.

The Dandie Dinmont is a unique looking dog, and gives the

62

appearance of having a head far too big for the comparatively small body which stands about 28 cm (11 in) at the shoulder. In effect, and for your rough guidance, he is of similar structure to the Sealyham and Scottish Terrier. The coat is outstanding and consists of soft silky hair, which is bunched on the top of the head, giving the somewhat unusual appearance. The colouring is usually blueish grey or silver grey, though sometimes it is fawn or light brown in colour. The jaws are very strong, and this breed is quite used to killing vermin, although in present times he has been more popularised for the show ring and as an attractive pet for the home. The body is long and curved over the loins, and the tail also curved slightly upward. He is powerfully built for a small dog, weighing about 7 kg (16 lb) and is increasing all the time in popularity. As a breed it would be safe to say that he is uncommon, and the average layman would have some difficulty in naming him on sight. As a small breed one can find nothing in his disfavour except perhaps that it is necessary to keep his coat in good condition, which means very regular and constant attention. The Dandie might well be your choice if you require a small, outstanding and aristocratic little dog.

Doberman   Illustration from Duphar's Kavak dog chart.

Bred as a guard dog in Germany, this strongly-built, large dog stands about 69 cm (27 in) high. It has a smooth, short coat which should be highly glossy; the colours are black and tan, brown and tan or blue and tan. It is a powerful dog, quick and alert in its movements, and demanding a lot of exercise. They are highly intelligent but need firm training. They are most suitable as a country dog.

Elkhound

This is a hardy sporting dog with very strong hunting instincts. The body is compact and proportionately short, the coat thick and abundant but not bristling. The head is broad, with a moderately long muzzle, and prick ears, set high. Legs are firm, straight and powerful, and the hind legs should look straight when viewed from behind. The tail is set high, and tightly curled over the back. The hair is coarse, thick and close. In colour it can be various greys, with black tips to the long outer coat; but too light or too dark colourings are not good for showing, nor are pronounced markings on legs and paws. Height is about 48 cm (19 in) and weight average is about 21 kg (46 lb).

English Springer Spaniel

This breed is related to the Cocker Spaniel, but is a slightly larger, heavier dog and marginally less popular. Bred as a gun dog, it has been recognised for almost two hundred years. It is one of the larger spaniels, growing to about 51 cm (20 in) at the shoulder and weighing on average 23 kg (50 lb). It is a powerfully-built, but compact dog with a long muscular neck and broad muzzle. The coat is straight, usually brown and white but sometimes black and white or tricolour. It is a strong and active dog, intelligent and a good companion, and therefore ideal as a pet.

The Welsh Springer Spaniel is a slightly lighter, smaller dog with a longer, less broad muzzle and short ears. Another working dog, it is lively, active and tireless.

Field Spaniel

Illustration from Duphar's Kavak dog chart.

The Field Spaniel was only recognised as a separate breed from the Cocker Spaniel in 1892, but is much less popular than the Cocker. It is a strong, compact dog; weighs about 22.5 kg (50 lb); and is about 46 cm (18 in) high. The coat is generally brown, or sometimes black, and is thick and glossy. The dark eyes and docile expression show that this is a quiet, affectionate dog which makes an excellent companion. It is particularly good with children.

Fox Terrier, Wire and Smooth

Illustration from Duphar's Kavak dog chart.

The only outstanding difference between the two breeds is the coat, which is decisive in each case. As in the case of the Scottish Terrier,

65

the Wire Fox Terrier has a very hard and wiry coat which will need stripping regularly. He is an extremely popular little dog, and game for anything; his colouring is attractive and he usually has a white background with black or tan markings; his weight should be 7 to 8 kg (16 to 18 lb). He should be fairly long in the head and have a good square jaw, which may be shown off to perfection when he has been trimmed and groomed, the beard being left intact. These are very upstanding little dogs, and from a show point of view the coat is considered a very important point. Without hesitation the Wire Fox Terrier may be accepted as an ideal companion house dog. In the event of choosing a puppy, ensure that he has ample width between the ears: though the head should not be wide there must be ample space for brain development, and a number of this breed have been bred far too narrow in this respect.

Foxhound
Illustration from Duphar's Kavak dog chart.

This is essentially a hunting dog, and is not often found in the ordinary household. For one thing it needs a considerable amount of meat and exercise to keep in good condition. English Foxhounds have been widely exported, and there is an American Foxhound Club. Colour is usually described as 'hound marking', which means a white background with broken markings of lemon, liver or brown. Foxhounds are generally about 61 cm (24 in) tall.

German Shepherd Dog

Illustration from Duphar's Kavak dog chart.

This breed is among the first half-dozen most popular dogs in Britain. He is otherwise known as the Alsatian, hailing from Alsace in Germany where he was used in a working capacity with great success. Although the breed has the appearance of the Wolf, there is no breed connection in any way, as so often supposed. In a way his appearance is his handicap as, quite wrongly, many people are afraid of this dog, and he has on occasions been given bad publicity most undeservedly. Definitely this is one of the most intelligent breeds known to us, and with a great war record; in wartime many thousands of these dogs were used with great success by the Forces and have since been found of great use in serving with civil police forces, as guards in the industrial world, and as guide dogs for the blind. The standard height for the German Shepherd Dog is not more than 66 cm (26 in) at the shoulder; the frame is built in such a way as to ensure an easy movement, which is almost cat-like; the chest is deep, allowing plenty of room for the heart and lungs. The head is long and clean cut, giving an extremely sharp and intelligent look. These dogs have very acute hearing and smell, ears stand erect, and the eyes are almond-shaped and dark. Legs are perfectly straight, and the dog has big bone formation. Colours vary considerably, but among the most common are black and tan, sable, grey, fawn and black. There are also white Alsatians, but these are less popular.

Great Dane

Illustration from Duphar's Kavak dog chart.

A very big breed with a striking appearance, which cannot be confused with any other dog. He can stand 91 cm (36 in) high and weigh 63.5 kg (140 lb); bitches, of course, are a little smaller. Although he stands very high he has a power of strength; the head is long and the jaws massive; ears should be small and set high; the neck is long and arched; forelegs straight with good bone; hindquarters carry plenty of muscle. There are a variety of colourings including brindle, black, harlequin, fawn and blue. This dog is very trainable when young. Care should be taken when choosing a puppy to ensure complete absence of rickets. Owing to his great size, the Dane is not everyone's dog, but he has a fine temperament and given plenty of space will make a fine companion and guard dog. The ears are not cropped in the UK.

Greyhound

Illustration from Duphar's Kavak dog chart.

This dog is rarely kept by the ordinary household; he is primarily a sporting and racing dog. He stands about 71 cm (28 in) high, has a good, deep chest and an oblique shoulder blade. The hindquarters are strong and broad across. The hind legs are muscular and wide apart; forelegs should be short from knee to ground and hind legs from hock to ground, the length being in the upper part of the leg. The tail is long, tapering and nicely curved. The coat is fine, thick and close, and there is a great variety of colour in the breed, including black, blue, brindle, white and particolours, the majority of dogs having some white markings. He has been accepted for many centuries as one of the most graceful of all breeds, elegant but full of muscular power.

Irish Terrier

Illustration from Duphar's Kavak dog chart.

The Irish Terrier is well known as being a very brave little dog. While he has a very strong character, he is a perfect companion and house pet. His weight should be over 11 kg (25 lb), which makes him a little heavier than the Fox Terrier, his height is about 46 cm (18 in); his colouring is usually of a reddy tan, and sometimes wheaten red; he has a short, hard, wiry coat, which does not require a lot of attention beyond a good regular brushing with a stiff brush. His stance is very upright; he has straight front legs with a neck inclined to be long; the skull is flat and the ears V-shaped. He is a popular terrier, though he has probably slightly diminished in numbers during recent years, for some unaccountable reason. He is well worth every consideration for your choice among the smaller dogs, particularly if you are looking for a good guard and companion. He is loyal and intelligent, and always responsive to training. Irish Terriers enjoy car travel, and are excellent with children.

Irish Water Spaniel　　　　Illustration from Duphar's Kavak dog chart.

This delightful-looking, large spaniel is distinguishable by his unusual coat which is long and curly with a curly topknot and a smooth face and tail. As the name suggests, this hunting dog was used to retrieve water fowl, so its coat is water resistant. An enthusiastic and strongly-built working dog, the Water Spaniel needs a great deal of exercise and can become boisterous if its lifestyle is not sufficiently active. It loves swimming, and this makes the coat easier to groom, although this is always a time-consuming and essential job for the dog owner. The colour of the coat should be a rich liver. The dog has a powerful frame, stands about 58 cm (23 in) high, and is most suited to a life in the country.

Irish Wolfhound　　　　Illustration from Duphar's Kavak dog chart.

Great size is a criterion for a well-bred specimen; and this is therefore a countryman's choice. He is the tallest of all dogs, very muscular, strong but graceful, easy and active in movement, and of commanding appearance. The head and neck are carried high, and the tail with an upward sweep and a slight curve towards the extremity. Minimum height is 79 cm (31 in) and weight 54 kg (120 lb) for a dog, rather less for a bitch. The muzzle is long and fairly pointed; the skull not too broad. The neck is long and well arched, without any loose skin about the throat. The hair is very rough and wiry, long over the eyes and under the jaw. The recognised colours include grey, brindle, red, black, pure white and fawn. Forelegs must be straight, and the ears must be carried like those of a Greyhound, not hanging flat to the face.

Keeshond   Illustration from Duphar's Kavak dog chart.

This breed shares a title with our little friend the Schipperke, both being known as Dutch Barge Dogs. The Keeshond is a most attractive animal; he is compact in size and has a very foxy appearance, prick ears and alert features. He is of medium build and can easily be confused with the Elkhound by the layperson, which in the circumstances is a forgivable error. His height should not exceed 46 cm (18 in). He has a thick bushy coat of a sable colouring or wolf marking; the muzzle, legs and tail are of a slightly lighter shade. His counterpart in Germany, the Wolfspitz, is a bigger dog. In Holland the Keeshond does vary a little in size, down to dogs of the Pomeranian size, which he resembles in points. Ears are erect, and the breed is very sensitive to the slightest sound; this makes them excellent guard dogs, and of course, they are used for this express purpose in the canals, for protecting barges and their contents. He is quite a popular dog in Britain, but is usually just enough bigger than the terrier family to make him not entirely suitable for the flat or small house.

Kerry Blue Terrier

Illustration from Duphar's Kavak dog chart.

This breed has gained great prominence during the past twenty years, though it cannot yet be termed everyman's dog as can some of the more popular terriers. As with so many breeds we have described, the strong point of the Kerry Blue is his coat: it is usually blue in colour, sometimes various related shades, and on occasions almost appears black; it is very soft in texture, and he carries an attractive fringe over the eyes. The dog weighs between 14 and 16 kg (30 and 35 lb) and is of very solid build. The head is long and the jaw very strong; the body is of medium length and level; all four legs are strong and muscular, and he is the type of dog that would give an intruder a very bad time, which makes him ideal for a house guard and companion. If you decide to choose this breed, go to one of the good specialist breeders, many of whom you will meet at the average dog show, and learn more about them. This is in my opinion a very fine dog, and one might well be proud to own one.

King Charles Spaniel

As the name indicates, the breed goes back to the period of Charles II, when these dogs were the King's firm favourites. The colourings are black and tan, tricolour, ruby and Blenheim. Show points for the four varieties are the same. This is a small spaniel, and low to the ground, average weight being 4.5 kg (10 lb); the skull is very big and well-domed, the nose short and turned up; the ears are long and hang low, carrying long hair; eyes are wide apart. The coat is long and silky and bears the same feathering as the others of the spaniel family. The most popular colours appear to be the black and tan and the tricolour, the former being glossy black with bright tan markings, and the latter a background of white with patches of black and tan markings. Some years ago a pack of this breed was kept for hunting in Britain. This dog will well suit the connoisseur and yet will fit into the average home, looking every bit the aristocrat.

Manchester Terrier　　　　　　Illustration from Duphar's Kavak dog chart.

The Manchester Terrier gained its name from its popularity in that area of Britain as a ratter, both in the countryside and also in the dog ring, where the men used to gamble on the number of rats their dog could kill in a given time. It has a smooth, short coat which maintains a natural gloss and is trouble-free in maintenance. The colour is black and rich tan, the pattern of colouring usually being uniform. The Manchester Terrier is about 41 cm (16 in) high. The head should be long, flat and narrow with tapering jaws; eyes are small and dark, set fairly close together; ears are usually semi-erect. The neck is long and tapers from the shoulders to the head. The body is short and raised slightly at the loins. Legs must be quite straight and fairly long. The tail should be carried straight and be of moderate length.

The English Toy Terrier, or Miniature Black and Tan Terrier as it is sometimes called, is a very small edition of the Manchester Terrier. It is a very tiny dog indeed and frequently turns the scale at less than 3 kg (7 lb), being about 30 cm (12 in) high. Its characteristics are similar to the larger breed. It makes an excellent house dog, particularly where space is limited.

Mastiff

Illustration from Duphar's Kavak dog chart.

This has a greater history than most of our British breeds, and in recent years has so diminished in numbers as to cause grave concern in the dog world. Here again we have a large breed that cannot be everyone's choice, and he is a dog that fits rather into the large country home. History tells us that the breed was found in Britain by the Romans and that many were dispatched back to Rome for fighting in the arena with other animals; indeed we do know that they were used in Britain for bull baiting. The dog is massive rather than big in bulk form; he has a broad square head, short tan coat, small ears, very broad chest and a powerful body. He makes a formidable guard and companion, and there are few intruders who would advance even upon sight of such a dog. The Mastiff is a costly dog to purchase, and has a very healthy appetite. The average home could not unfortunately entertain a dog this size, the minimum height being 76 cm (30 in), though he does not require as much exercise as his bulk indicates.

The Bullmastiff is often confused with the Mastiff, but is derived from a cross with the Bulldog, though little of the latter shows itself today beyond the head features. The dog is slightly smaller than the Mastiff, 66 to 71 cm (26 to 28 in) at the shoulder, and weighs upwards of 41 kg (90 lb), a very solid build. The coat is short and usually fawn colour with a dark mask; the head is square with a fair amount of wrinkle; ears are V-shaped and set well back, the muzzle is square and deep, the whole dog is very muscular and has a wide, deep chest. A popular breed but probably not for the average household.

Old English Sheepdog Illustration from Duphar's Kavak dog chart.

This breed is part of the English way of life in more ways than one, and is an extremely popular breed. The outstanding feature is the coat, which is usually blue-grey in colour and long and shaggy; it calls for a lot of attention to look its best, with unlimited grooming. The size of the dog does vary, and it would be safe to say that the smaller type is used for shepherding and the larger variety for showing. Most dogs are upwards of 63 cm (25 in) at the shoulders. Although the Old English would be described as a big dog, one is surprised on seeing one cropped of his coat, and realising the enormous covering he possesses. The breed is very hardy and full of energy. The eyes are a dark colour and are seldom visible through the thick hair covering the face; the skull and jaw are square, and the head rather long and narrow; forelegs solid and straight, with feet small and round; the tail should be docked; the body is short and compact. Plenty of these dogs are still used with sheep but they would hardly be recognised against their well-groomed show ring cousins. This is not a breed for the average home, although a great favourite and with very high intelligence; he would be rather a handful for the housewife on a wet day. A dog of this type obviously belongs in the country.

Papillon

Illustration from Duphar's Kavak dog chart.

This elegant and attractive little French dog, standing only about 28 cm (11 in) high, has gained in popularity in recent years, although it is still fairly unusual. It is a friendly, energetic dog which loves attention. The long, silky coat is white with either red or black markings, heavily fringed with a plumed tail. Regular and careful grooming is essential. It gets the name Papillon, meaning 'butterfly', from the shape of its ears, which are carried erect and have a long, silky fringe.

Pekingese

Illustration from Duphar's Kavak dog chart.

Easily the most popular of the toy breeds, and standing very high on the whole breeds list, the Pekingese has an interesting history, which is mentioned on page 42. He has always drawn a very big entry at all dog shows, and is a firm favourite with the ladies. This is an extremely intelligent little dog, and small trouble to maintain. His beauty lies mainly in the coat, which is thick and long. He has a big head and flat, wrinkled muzzle. Maximum weight is 5.5 kg (12 lb). Legs are short, and the front ones bowed. The dog carries feathering on thighs, legs, tail and feet. It has a heavy mane, and a frill under the neck. The tail is carried right over the back. Colouring is varied. This is a delightful little dog, which will undoubtedly always be in popular demand.

Pinscher, Miniature

Illustration from Duphar's Kavak dog chart.

The full-sized German Pinscher was one of the breeds used as foundation stock for the Doberman, but is now a much less common breed and rarely seen. The Miniature Pinscher is becoming increasingly popular, however, as it is an energetic and intelligent dog which makes an ideal companion. It has the advantage of its small size, about 30 cm (12 in) high, which makes it an ideal house dog even for smaller homes. The smooth coat, black and tan or red, is short, glossy and trouble-free in maintenance. Like the Chihuahua, this small dog makes an excellent guard as it has acute hearing and a penetrating bark which it uses to good effect if it detects an unusual disturbance.

Pointer

Illustration from Duphar's Kavak dog chart.

This is one of larger sporting breeds, a magnificent dog, extremely popular in the country particularly with gamekeepers. He has an acute hearing and keen sense of smell, which perfects him for his work. In no way can the pointer be described as a domestic dog. This does not mean that he has anything but a perfect temperament, and he is a great friend of man, but he is lost without the country. The Scottish country and moorland suit his capabilities. As his name indicates, he will 'point' game, and also drive. He has German counterparts, the Wire-Haired and Short-Haired Pointers, and it is said that these types originally hailed from Spain. He is a very powerful dog with plenty of staying power, which is necessary for field work. He is normally liver and mottled white in colour; he has a long head and neck, the latter being very muscular; ears are of medium length and fine and silky; his coat is short and has a fine sheen on it. He is an attractive dog and stands about 66 cm (26 in) at the shoulder. A breed to be recommended for the stable or farm rather than the domestic fireside.

Pointer, German Illustration from Duphar's Kavak dog chart.

Another excellent working dog, this German breed is well known for its courage and tenacity. It is a very popular gun dog both in Germany and in other European countries but is less popular in Britain. It has a stockier build than the Pointer, with a larger head and thicker muzzle; the forelegs are straight and the body solid and muscular. He is normally liver and mottled white in colour.

Pointer, German Short-Haired Illustration from Duphar's Kavak dog chart.

Another German breed, the Short-Haired Pointer was bred as a gun dog, and it has the usual qualities of a working dog: strong build, stamina, speed and a good nose. He is normally liver and mottled white, like the Pointer, but is sometimes solid liver, black or white. His head is broader than the Pointer, but he shares the muscular neck and powerful build. The height is 64 cm (25 in) on average. The coat is short and lies flat to the body. The Short-Haired Pointer is a good working dog, and not suitable for most homes.

Pomeranian　　　　　　　　　Illustration from Duphar's Kavak dog chart.

The breed at one time was the favourite of toy dogs, and they are still extremely popular, commanding an above-average price. When they were first introduced into Britain, they were white in colour, and considerably bigger than the present-day specimen. There is little doubt they are related to some of the Scandinavian breeds, and have been bred down in size. A number of colours have been introduced by specialists, the usual one being a foxy red; some of the smaller ones weigh less than 2 kg (4 lb). This is a very neat little dog with a very sharp fox-like appearance; the small ears are erect, and the body short and compact. The coat is long and fluffy with a prominent neck ruffle; the tail lies flat over the back and is well covered with long hair; the feet are small and neat. This is another breed whose coat requires a great deal of attention to look its best, and can be seen to advantage at all dog shows, where the breed always enjoys a prominent entry.

Poodle

Illustration from Duphar's Kavak dog chart.

This is a breed that is particularly popular as a town dog. The Poodle is a fine companion, and in spite of his rather unusual appearance is very intelligent. There is no doubt that owners get a lot of pleasure in having their Poodle clipped in one of the recognised forms. He has a rather long, well-shaped head, a long muzzle and fairly long and wide ears. He carries his head high, and the body is compact and slightly hollowed. Front legs are straight, the feet small, and the tail is carried high and straight. The coat is very thick and of a hard texture. Colours vary from black to white, and silver to apricot, the latter being more costly.

The Miniature Poodle is now being bred as small as possible, one reason being that, as a town dog, he is easily picked up and tucked under the arm. The characteristics are the same as the standard Poodle, but the height is less than 38 cm (15 in).

The Toy Poodle is even smaller, the recognised height being less than 28 cm (11 in) high.

Pug

Illustration from Duphar's Kavak dog chart.

Originally bred in China, the Pug was brought to Britain in the seventeenth century, and is now an extremely popular town dog, being small, intelligent, alert and easy to look after. The distinctive feature of the Pug is his head, which is large with a foreshortened muzzle, a heavily wrinkled face and large, dark eyes. The mask is black while the rest of the coat is fawn; it is smooth and short and requires very little maintenance. A stocky little dog, the Pug weighs up to 8 kg (18 lb), has a solid, muscular body, a thick neck and a tightly curled tail.

Pyrenean Mountain Dog

Illustration from Duphar's Kavak dog chart.

This huge, white dog is similar in appearance to the better-known St Bernard and is therefore unsuitable for most families because of his vast size, usually over 76 cm (30 in). Bred to protect the flocks of sheep on the Pyrenean mountains from attack by wolves, he is still an excellent guard dog, but needs careful training as he is inclined to be of an independent nature. His coat is thick and white, sometimes with darker markings of grey or brown, and the legs are feathered. He is solidly built, with a thick neck and large head.

Retriever, Golden

Illustration from Duphar's Kavak dog chart.

This is a handsome, powerful dog, highly intelligent and easy to teach. The eyes are wide apart, small, dark and gentle in expression. Forelegs are perfectly straight, the hocks well bent and placed low to the ground. The outer coat is flat or wavy (not curly), and there is feather on thighs, tail and forelegs. The colour at its best is a rich golden red; average weight is 36 kg (80 lb); average height is 61 cm (24 in). His size makes the Retriever a dog for the country, but by nature he makes a good friend of the family.

Retriever, Labrador

Illustration from Duphar's Kavak dog chart.

This is an increasingly popular breed, strongly built, active and with great powers of endurance. He differs in appearance from the Golden Retriever, his head being a little broader and chest wider. The coat is short, thick and without wave; colour may be black, yellow or red, although the former is the most common. The jaws are powerful and long, but not exaggerated in length. The wide skull gives plenty of 'brain room'. Eyes are brown, yellow or black. The height is about 56 cm (22 in).

St Bernard

Illustration from Duphar's Kavak dog chart.

This is one of the biggest known breeds and a very noble and handsome dog. By virtue of his size there are but few homes in this country that could house such a dog in comfort, to say nothing of the high cost of his food. These dogs have been bred at the St Bernard Hospice on the Great St Bernard Pass for some centuries; in the capable hands of the monks they have performed many great errands of mercy in saving travellers lost in the snowy wastes of the pass. The dog is not used in any working capacity in this country, though from personal experience I would say he is definitely trainable. He has a huge head with a square muzzle, and the colouring is a very attractive one, tan, chestnut and white in broken formation both on the body and head. He is a very upstanding dog, the forelegs being straight and with large feet; the dog should stand about 91 cm (36 in) at the shoulder. The coat is thick and flat with some feather on the legs. A good specimen must be well proportioned and big in all respects. A St Bernard is a costly proposition, and while he is among the uncommon breeds there are a good number of breeders and exhibitors in Britain, and the dog always enjoys a prominent place at the big shows.

Saluki, or Gazelle Hound   Illustration from Duphar's Kavak dog chart.

This is a dog that needs a home in the country. His whole appearance is one of grace and symmetry, great activity, speed, strength and endurance. The coat is smooth and silky, and the slight feather on the legs, at the back of the thigh, and sometimes on thigh and shoulders is generally associated with this breed: there is, however, a smooth variety, the only distinguishing feature of which is the lack of feather. Average height for a dog is about 66 cm (26 in), but the bitch may be considerably smaller. The head is long and narrow, but the skull is moderately broad between the ears; the nose is black or liver-coloured. Forelegs are straight and long from elbow to knee. Hindquarters are strong, with hip bones wide apart, hocks low to the ground. The dog is built for running and jumping. The tail is long, set on low, and carried in a curve.

Samoyed   Illustration from Duphar's Kavak dog chart.

The Samoyed is still a relatively unusual breed in Britain, but its popularity has increased over recent years because of its striking appearance and affectionate nature. It is a large, heavily built dog standing about 56 cm (22 in) high and weighing about 25 kg (55 lb). Although the coat looks silky, it is in fact thick and coarse with a soft undercoat, as it was designed to protect the dog from the Russian weather when the dogs were used to herd reindeer. The tail is thick and curled, the forelegs straight and feathered, and the dog has a thick ruff round the neck. The coat is white, cream or biscuit-coloured and must be groomed regularly and thoroughly. It was originally bred for stamina, so needs a good deal of exercise. They are good with children and love to play, being especially fond of a romp in the snow.

Schnauzer   Illustration from Duphar's Kavak dog chart.

Its unusual appearance with its attractive long eyebrows and whiskers as well as its intelligent nature make this increasingly popular dog a great companion. A medium-sized dog about 48 cm (19 in) high, it is thickset and muscular with straight forelegs, a thick, straight neck and the characteristic square-looking muzzle with its long whiskers. The ears are V-shaped, set on high and drop forwards. The most common colouring is grey with some black or white markings, but black is also popular. The Schnauzer looks his best when professionally trimmed, and the slightly coarse coat is then easy to maintain. The beard and legs need to be washed regularly, but otherwise these dogs seldom need bathing.

The Miniature Schnauzer is a high-spirited, companionable little dog which is ideal for the smaller home, as it is less than 36 cm (14 in) high, lively, affectionate and easy to look after. Intelligent and simple to train, it has a penetrating bark which makes it a good guard dog.

Scottish Deerhound

Illustration from Duphar's Kavak dog chart.

This large, aristocratic-looking dog was bred with the strength and speed needed to chase and fell deer in the Scottish Highlands. It is very much a countryman's dog as it needs a great deal of exercise. The blue-grey coat is wiry and weather-resistant; the dog weighs up to 48 kg (105 lb) and is about 76 cm (30 in) high. It is an intelligent and loyal dog, but unsuitable for most families.

Scottish Terrier

Illustration from Duphar's Kavak dog chart.

The Scottish Terrier is truly a representative product of Scotland and he is exceptionally popular the world over. He is a game little dog and very solidly built; he has a short, hard, wiry coat which is black in colour, and it is customary to have the coat stripped twice a year as its growth is very profuse. His weight should be in the region of 8 kg (18 lb). He has short legs; his head is long and the jaw strong; ears are small and erect; the neck is short and thickset. The tail is not docked. The Scottish Terrier, or Aberdeen as he is sometimes known, is a fine little house dog in every way. He is a great sportsman and afraid of nothing. He is certainly among the most popular breeds in the dog world.

Sealyham

This breed has gained prominence in a comparatively short space of time. They are very game little dogs and will tackle anything on four legs if necessary. They have little or no resemblance to any of the other terriers. They are mostly white in colour, with usually a lemon or brown patch on the head or on the back and ears; the body is low, set on very short legs, and the best height is close to 25 cm (10 in) at the shoulder; the body is thickset, with a broad, deep chest; the head fairly wide, and the jaws powerful; the neck is long and thick. He is certainly well built for digging out vermin; he is a great sport and very tenacious, and considering his very short legs can stand a great deal of exercise. Some specimens are definitely more cobbly than others, and there is also a noticeable difference in the head size of some strains. The Sealyham cannot possibly be mistaken for any other breed, and I think it is possibly their greatest gameness that appeals to the dog lover. You should give a Sealyham puppy every consideration if you have a modest-sized house and a large garden and children.

Setter, English

This is a beautiful relative of the spaniel, and both an excellent gun dog and a good companion. He is built for running and for doing a long day's work. Feet must be close and compact, with hair between the toes. The head is long and lean, the skull oval between the ears, with plenty of 'brain room'. The dark hazel eyes, bright, mild and intelligent, are a good index to the dog's character. The ears are set on low, are of moderate length, and hang in folds close to the cheek. The tail is carried almost on a line with the back. The long and silky coat is slightly wavy, and there is plenty of feather on legs and tail. Colour varies but is generally white with flicks of black or orange; weight is up to 30 kg (66 lb); height about 64 cm (25 in). The English Setter makes an excellent pet as it is particularly affectionate and thrives on human company.

Setter, Gordon
Illustration from Duphar's Kavak dog chart.

The Gordon Setter makes a delightful companion as he is intelligent, gentle, loyal and hard working. He was originally bred by the Dukes of Gordon for hunting grouse on the Scottish moors, so is powerfully built with plenty of stamina. About the same height as the English Setter, the Gordon Setter has a muscular body and a thick neck; the skull and muzzle are broad and the eyes are dark and gentle in expression. The wavy black and tan coat is silky and lies flat to the body with feathers on the legs and tail, which is carried almost on a line with the back. Provided he has adequate space and exercise, the Gordon has an excellent temperament for a house dog.

Setter, Irish Red

Illustration from Duphar's Kavak dog chart.

The most distinctive characteristic is the colour, which should be a rich, deep red. He may have white on the chest, throat or toes, a small star on the forehead, or a narrow blaze on the nose or face, but this is not desirable. Otherwise he closely resembles his cousins, the English and Gordon Setters. His medium to dark coloured eyes have a soft expression which is a good indication of his sweet, affectionate and fun loving temperament.

Shetland Sheepdog

Illustration from Duphar's Kavak dog chart.

It is only relatively recently that these very popular little dogs have partly left their working life to enjoy a domestic one. In the Isles of their origin they are of a rougher type, and of course used solely for working. Their standard of intelligence is outstanding. Some of the smaller types measure only 30 cm (12 in) at the shoulder, being bred for show. The coat should be long with a generous frill, and colouring is usually lemon and white, though many broken colours are admissible. The legs are feathered and the tail carried down with an upward curl at the tip; the skull is flat and the nose long and tapering; eyes are almond-shaped and brown in colour; ears are small and carried half erect. This dog has a deep chest and straight forelegs. He is very hardy, as indeed he must be, and enjoys a very considerable popularity largely thanks to the fancier. It is seldom one can use the word pretty to describe a working dog, but it certainly applies to the 'Sheltie'.

Skye Terrier   Illustration from Duphar's Kavak dog chart.

Unfortunately this is not among the most popular terriers in this country. The Skye Terrier is very much an individual dog, being unlike most of the other terriers in appearance; the great feature is the coat, which is very long and flat, and covers the forehead and eyes; the tail is feathered; the body is long and low, only about 25 cm (10 in) high. The ears are usually pricked, though they may be longer and pendulant; the head is long and the skull fairly wide; the back is level, with a very slight drop from the flanks to the shoulder. He is by average standards a fairly costly purchase but offsets this by his extremely economical maintenance; he has a very strong bark for such a small dog, and will certainly let you know if there is anyone about.

Weimaraner   Illustration from Duphar's Kavak dog chart.

The Weimaraner is a real aristocrat of the dog world. The German aristocratic sportsmen who originally bred these dogs wanted an exclusive-looking breed which also had all the best qualities of the sporting breeds. This superb, tall dog, standing up to 69 cm (27 in) high, with its silken grey coat was the result. It is a large, strong dog with straight forelegs, large ears and pale blue-grey or amber eyes. Some dogs have small white markings on the chest, but any other markings are not desirable. It needs space and exercise, and is friendly and obedient but must be properly trained by a firm handler. It is really only suitable as a working dog and not as a pet, as it always needs a useful role to play.

Welsh Corgi Illustration from Duphar's Kavak dog chart.

There are two varieties of this breed, namely the Pembroke and the Cardiganshire, and as the names indicate they hail from those parts of the Welsh country, where they have been used extensively for herding cattle, these little dogs keeping the beasts moving by nipping them in the hocks. The Pembroke is a small breed and should weigh around 9 kg (20 lb). He has a very foxy appearance and the coat is short and thick, usually red in colour or red and white. He is a stocky little dog standing on short legs; he has a sharp appearance with a rather snippy nose, the skull being wide between the ears; the chest is broad and deep, particularly between the front legs; the body is fairly long, the tail short and stumpy, and the ears carried erect. (Illustration above.)

The Cardigan has a long tail, which is the outstanding point of difference between the two varieties, otherwise their overall size is much the same. The Corgi is a great present-day favourite, and the Royal Family have been greatly instrumental in the matter, this little dog being a great favourite of Queen Elizabeth. Their present popularity is also in no small measure due to the way they fit into the average home with little or no trouble.

Welsh Terrier

Illustration from Duphar's Kavak dog chart.

The Welsh Terrier could be described as the miniature Airedale, though really he is quite in a class of his own, and one of the favourites of the big terrier family. For the purpose of guidance in size, he compares with the Fox Terrier. His coat is very wiry and is usually black and tan in colour with a satin-like sheen. He needs periodical trimming, but otherwise his coat is relatively easy to look after. He has a flat, rather wide head with a powerful jaw, small V-shaped ears carried high, together with small eyes; his back is short and he is fairly wide for his size; he has straight front legs and small feet, and weighs in all very close to 9 kg (20 lb). The breed enjoys a greater prominence in the west and north part of Britain; he is an ideal dog for the average home, being a good companion, trouble-free, and economical to maintain. The Welsh Terrier can hold his own in ratting with any breed and is still used in this capacity in many parts of Britain.

West Highland White Terrier

Illustration from Duphar's Kavak dog chart.

This breed should be very much more popular than it is today. He is a delightful little dog, completely white in colour, and in stature rather resembles the Cairn Terrier. He should weigh about 7 kg (16 lb), is stockily built, with a deep chest, straight back, and plenty of muscle. He is a very strong little dog, being bred for working, in ratting and seeking out other small vermin. He has a foxy head, which is rather short, and powerful jaws, small prick ears, and a tail that should be approximately 15 cm (6 in) long. The legs are short and the hocks bent and set under the body; the coat is hard and of medium length; although it should be pure white it is sometimes of a creamy colouring.

The breed enjoys considerable prominence at the shows, but I should like to see more of them owned by 'the man in the street', and reach a population to compete with the Scottish Terrier. The West Highland is a very sharp little dog for the home and a good companion; strangely enough, many people dislike white dogs for the obvious reason, but it is rather a pity in this case, as we have here a breed altogether unique in character. It is even-tempered, loves company and responds well to training.

Whippet　　　　　　　　Illustration from Duphar's Kavak dog chart.

This dog enjoys outstanding popularity in the north of England, where coursing is popular. It is built for speed, with long legs, strong and broad hindquarters, and hocks low to the ground. The tops of the shoulder-blades should be fairly close together. The head is long and lean, flat at the top and rather wide between the eyes. Eyes are bright, alert and fiery; ears small, fine in texture, and carried half erect, not bolt upright. The chest must be deep and capacious, with plenty of 'heart room'. The long tapering tail should not be carried higher than the level of the back when the dog is in action. Colour may be black, blue, red, fawn, brindle, white or mixtures of these. The dewclaws should be removed when a puppy is a few days old. Average height is about 46 cm (18 in) and weigh about 9 kg (20 lb). Affectionate and easy to manage, the Whippet makes an ideal dog for the home.

Yorkshire Terrier

Despite his very small size, the Yorkshire Terrier can hold his own with considerably larger breeds. He has a very strong character for such a tiny dog and is very much liked as a house pet, being small enough to curl easily into one's lap. The coat is of abnormal length, and consequently needs a great deal of grooming right from birth; as the hair grows after the first few months, the coat should be kept oiled with, for preference, the finest olive oil; it hangs evenly down each side of the body with a parting in the centre from nose to tail. The hair should be fine and glossy and grey-blue in colour, with a rich tan head and similar leg and chest markings. The puppies are actually born black and tan, and undergo a change of colour after a few months. The body is compact and level, legs straight and hairy, feet round, and tail docked to medium length; the head is small and rather flat, and muzzle of medium length. The Yorkshire Terrier is an ideal dog for the elderly person with limited accommodation; for he is not only a great companion, but very sharp-witted and has a keen sense of hearing.

Index

Numbers in italics refer to illustrations.

Aberdeen Terrior *see*
   Scottish Terrier
Afghan Hound 49, *49*
Airedale Terrier 48,
   49–50, *49*, 92
Alsatian *see* German
   Shepherd Dog

ball, rubber 16
basket 12, 13, 14, 19, 47
Basset Hound 50, *50*
bath 37
Beagle 51, *51*
Bedlington Terrier
   51–52, *51*
Bernese Mountain Dog
   52
biscuits 18, 26, 28, 29,
   47
Black and Tan Terrier,
   Miniature 73
Bloodhound 44, 52–53,
   52
bones 16, 29
   rubber 12, 16
Border Collie *see* Collie
Border Terrier 53, *53*
Borzoi 42, 48, 54, *54*
Boston Terrier 55, *55*
bowl, drinking 15, *15*,
   47
   feeding 15, *15*, 47
box 12, *13*, 47
Boxer 55, *55*
breeder 7, 17, 18
breeding 40, 41
   bitches 40, 47
bronchitis 35
brush 16, *16*
Bull Terrier 55, 56, *56*
Bulldog 55, 56–57, *56*, 74
Bullmastiff 74

Cairn Terrier 57, *57*, 92
car sickness 31
caster oil 35
cats 24, *24*
Chihuahua 58, *58*, 77
children 6, 24

chill 34
Chow-Chow 58, *58*
Clumber Spaniel 59
coat 15, *15*, 35, 47
Cocker Spaniel 10, 26,
   27, 56, 59, *59*, 64,
   65
colds 34, 35
collar 14, 15, *15*, 47
Collie, Border 59–60,
   59
   Rough 60, *60*
   Smooth 60
comb 16, *16*
conditioner 27
constipation 27, 35
Corgi *see* Welsh Corgi
cross-breed 8, 10, 11

Dachshund 5, 26
   Long-Haired 61
   Miniature 61
   Smooth-Haired 61,
   61
Dalmatian 11, 62, *62*
Dandie Dinmont 51,
   62–63, *62*
diarrhoea 35
distemper 35
Doberman 63, *63*, 77
Deerhound, Scottish
   86, *86*

eczema 36
Elkhound 64, *64*, 71
English Toy Terrier 73
exercise 19, 26, 29, 30,
   35

feeding 17, 19, 28
Field Spaniel 59, 65, *65*
Fox Terrier 55, 69, 92
   Smooth 65–66, *65*
   Wire 10, 65–66, *65*
Foxhound 51, 66, *66*

gastro-enteritis 35
Gazelle Hound *see*
   Saluki

German Shepherd Dog
   5, 7, 24, 26, 43, 44,
   45, 67, *67*
Great Dane 7, 68, *68*
Greyhound 42, 54,
   68–69, *68*, 71
grooming 16, *16*, 26, 27
guard dog 5, 7, 14, 43,
   44
guide dog 5, 45, 46, *46*,
   47
gun dog 8

harness 14, 21
Husky 43

illness 34–37
inoculation 35, 36, 39,
   47
Irish Terrier 69, *69*
Irish Water Spaniel 70,
   70
Irish Wolfhound 70–71,
   70

Keeshond 71, *71*
kennel 12, 13, *14*, 47
   boarding 38, 39, 47
   Club, English 10
   quarantine 38, 47
Kerry Blue Terrier 72,
   72
King Charles Spaniel
   59, 72–73, *72*

Labrador 11, 45
laxative 35
lead 14, 15, *15*, 21, 22,
   47
   slip 21
licence 18, 47
liquid paraffin 35

Manchester Terrier 73,
   73
mange, follicular 36, 37
   sarcoptic 36, 37
Mastiff 74, *74*
meat 17, 28, 47

milk 12, 17
minerals 28
mongrel *see* cross-breed

Newfoundland 43

Old English Sheepdog
  see Sheepdog

Papillon 76, *76*
parvo virus 35
pedigree 8, 10, 11
  form *9*
Pekingese 26, 42, 48,
  76, *76*
Pet shop 7
Pinscher 77
  Miniature 77, *77*
Pointer 77–78, *77*, *79*
  German 78, *78*
  German Short-Haired
  78–79, *78*
Pomeranian 71, 79, *79*
Poodle 42, 80, *80*
  Miniature 11, 80
  Toy 80
public transport 32
Pug 81, *81*
punishment 19
purgative 35
Pyrenean Mountain
  Dog 81, *81*

quarantine 38, 47

Retriever 46, 48
  Golden 82, *82*
  Labrador 82, *82*
roads 24

St Bernard 7, 30, 48, 81,
  83, *83*
Saluki 84, *84*
Samoyed 84–85, *84*
Schnauzer 85, *85*
  Miniature 85
Scottish Terrier 29, 57,
  63, 86, *86*
Sealyham 5, 63, 87, *87*
Setter 48
  English 87–88, *87*, 89
  Gordon 88, *88*, 89
  Irish Red 89, *89*
Sheepdog 43, 44, 48
  Old English 43, 75, *75*
  Welsh 43
  Scottish 43
  Shetland 48, 89–90,
  89
shows dog 6, 10
Skye Terrier 90, *90*
Spaniel 11, 42, 48, 87
  see also individual
  entries
Springer Spaniel
  English 5, 59, 64–65,
  64
  Welsh 59, 65
stripping 16, 27
  knife 16

Terrier 8, 17, 48 *see also*
  individual entries
toys 12
training 13, 19, 24
  house 17, 19
  obedience 20
  specialist 24, 43, 44,
  45
travelling 31–33

veterinary, certificate 10
  surgeon 8, 18, 27, 34,
  35, 36
vitamins 28

watch-dog 45
water 26, 30
  Spaniel, Irish, 70, *70*
Weimaraner 90–91, *90*
Welsh Corgi 11, 48, 91
  Cardiganshire *11*, 91
  Pembroke 91, *91*
Welsh Terrier 92, *92*
West Highland White
  Terrier 92–93, *92*
Whippet 93, *93*
Wolfhound, Irish 70–71,
  70
Wolfspitz 71
working dogs 43, 44, 45,
  46
worming 18, 37

Yorkshire Terrier 94, *94*